The Encounter

Sometimes,
God Has to Intervene

The Encounter

Stephen Arterburn

with James Pence

THOMAS NELSON
Since 1798

NASHVILLE   DALLAS   MEXICO CITY   RIO DE JANEIRO

Published in Nashville, Tennessee, by Thomas Nelson. Thomas Nelson is a registered trademark of Thomas Nelson, Inc.

Thomas Nelson, Inc. titles may be purchased in bulk for educational, business, fund-raising, or sales promotional use. For information, please e-mail SpecialMarkets@ThomasNelson.com.

Page design by Mark L. Mabry

Library of Congress Cataloging-in-Publication Data

Arterburn, Stephen, 1953-
  The encounter : sometimes God has to intervene / Stephen Arterburn.
     p. cm.
  ISBN 978-0-7852-3195-0 (trade paper)
  1. Forgiveness--Religious aspects--Christianity. 2. Providence and government of God--Christianity. I. Title.
  BV4647.F55A783 2011
  241'.4--dc23

                              2011025326

Printed in the United States of America

11 12 13 14 15 QG 5 4 3

To Gary Stump
So grateful to be ministering alongside you

Chapter One

How do you tear down a wall you've been building most of your life?

I looked out the window of my Gulfstream G650. It was the middle of the day, but you'd never guess that by looking at the sun. Alaska was progressing through the long polar night, and the periods of daylight were slowly growing longer, but the sun stayed close to the horizon most of the time.

My pilot's voice echoed through the cabin: "We've begun our descent into Fairbanks, Mr. Rush. We'll be on the ground in about twenty minutes."

What in the world am I doing here?

I enjoyed visiting Fairbanks. It's where I lived until I was nine. But I had spent the last twenty-six years in Miami, and my tolerance for the Arctic climate was considerably lower than it was during my youth.

January was definitely not the time for me to make this trip.

But I didn't have a choice. Not really.

"Jonathan, you've got to get to the bottom of this, and you have to do it *now*. It's eating you alive."

"You mean, just drop everything and jet off to Fairbanks?" I protested. "Just like that?"

Tim Moser, my counselor, was adamant. "Yes. Just like that."

"I can't just walk away and go off on some wild-goose chase," I told him.

Tim's face filled with concern. "Don't tell me you can't get away, Jon. If you don't, it's going to destroy you."

"What if I hired a private investigator? Wouldn't that be as good?"

Tim leaned back in his chair. "Jon, you came to me for advice, and I'm giving it. I think this is something you have to search out for yourself. I know you're great at delegating, but this is your task. No one else can do it."

I tried to think of other excuses, but couldn't muster anything. And now here I sat aboard my private jet, about to revisit the ghosts of my past in hopes of finding peace.

Realistically, peace was more than I could hope for.

And love?

I'd abandoned that hope long ago.

My driver, a tall young man who looked like he was in his twenties, stood in the terminal. He was holding a fur-lined parka.

I gave him a little wave. The gold name tag on his uniform said "Ryan."

"Welcome to Fairbanks, Mr. Rush."

I nodded and traded my briefcase for the parka. I glanced down at his feet, then at mine. My Italian loafers were definitely not the best choice of footwear, but I'd forgotten to ask him to bring a pair of bunny boots.

Too late now. I hope my feet won't freeze before I get to the limo.

"Right this way," he said.

As I followed Ryan toward the airport exit, a young woman came running up. She was short and disheveled, with curly blonde hair trailing down into her eyes.

"Mr. Rush," she said, "I'm Erica Bingham, a reporter for the *Daily News-Miner.* Could I ask you a few questions?"

I shook my head and kept walking.

She fell in step with me. "You know, it's not often our only local celebrity comes to town. Can't you spare a little time for an interview?"

"The last personal interview I gave was to Barbara Walters, and she had a tough time convincing me to do that one."

"Why is that?" Erica asked.

"I don't like reporters," I said.

She was undaunted. "Oh, come on. We're not all that bad."

"True," I said. "There are a few reporters I like, but it's a very short list."

"Could you at least confirm or deny the rumor?"

"Which one?"

"That Advanced Data Systems is planning to open a branch office here in Fairbanks."

I stopped and flashed a smile. "Do you know what I dislike worse than a reporter?"

She shook her head.

"A reporter who can't take no for an answer." I nodded to Ryan. "Let's go."

Ryan picked up my bags, and we headed for the terminal door. As we walked away, I felt a twinge of guilt. My pastor would not have approved of the way I had treated the reporter.

I don't suppose God approved either.

Old habits die hard.

Near the terminal door, my driver said, "Mr. Rush, if you'd prefer, you can wait inside the terminal while I get the limo."

I shook my head. "I can handle it."

When I followed Ryan out of the terminal, the cold air hit me like a baseball bat to the chest. I kept my mouth shut and breathed through my nose, but it didn't help much. After living most of my life in Florida, breathing Alaska's winter air was almost as bad as taking a polar bear jump into freezing water.

We made our way out to the limo, and I settled in the backseat while Ryan took care of my bags and then slid behind the wheel. I closed the partition between Ryan and me. He hadn't seemed overly chatty, but I didn't want to give him the chance to start. My business in Fairbanks was my own, and I wanted it to stay that way.

Ryan had barely pulled out of the airport parking lot when my BlackBerry chirped, signaling an incoming e-mail. I was surprised it had taken this long for someone from the office to contact me. They'd managed on their own a lot longer than I'd expected.

I pulled it out and looked at the sender. It wasn't from the office; it was from Tim.

The e-mail had only one line: "Have you written the letter?"

I sighed and wrote back, "Not yet."

Seconds later, the phone rang. I was tempted to let it go to voice mail, but I knew that Tim wouldn't let me off the hook that easily.

"Hi, Tim," I said, hoping that I didn't sound as guilty as I felt.

Tim got straight to the point. "So why haven't you written it?"

"I've been trying, but I can't find the words."

"Where do you get stuck?"

I hesitated a second and then said, "At 'Dear Mom.'"

"I never said it would be easy."

"You were right."

"This is important, Jonathan. Promise me you'll write the letter today."

"Tim, I—"

"Promise me."

I didn't reply for several seconds. Tim knew that although I had many faults, dishonesty was not among them. If he could get a promise out of me, he knew I'd be honor-bound to fulfill it.

After a few more seconds of silence, Tim's gentle but insistent voice broke through. "I'm waiting."

"All right," I said. "I promise. I'll do it before I go to bed tonight."

"Good." I could hear the satisfaction in his voice. "I'll call tomorrow to make sure you followed through."

"I'm sure you will," I said.

I smiled as I closed the phone. When Tim latched on to a reclamation project, he was like a pit bull. There was no letting up.

And it just so happened that I was his current project.

"Dear Mom."

I shook my head and scratched out the words. That wouldn't work.

"Mother."

That wouldn't work either.

I crumpled the paper and threw it into the trash can.

I couldn't explain it to Tim, but this was why I hadn't been able to write the letter. I didn't even know how to start. How do you write a letter to your mother when you don't know what to call her? When you don't even know her name? When you don't know the point of writing to her in the first place?

I tossed my pen onto the desk and walked over to the window. The lights of Fairbanks twinkled in the distance.

I wanted so badly to just go home and forget the whole thing. This was a crazy quest, an exercise in futility. But I promised Tim I'd follow through. And even if I were the kind of guy who breaks promises, I'd never break one to Tim. He had saved my life.

Crank it out, Jon, I told myself as I sat back down at the desk. *Just get something on paper, if for no other reason than to get Tim off your back.*

So I picked up my pen and began to write:

Dear person who gave birth to me,

I don't know what to call you. I don't know your name. And I don't feel right calling you Mother or Mom because you were neither of those things in my life. You did bring me into the world, and for that I guess I can thank you.

I don't remember what you look like. If I were to meet you on the street, I'd walk right past you. There are snatches of memories, but they are fleeting and cloudy.

But although I don't remember you, I do remember the day you left me.

It was the worst day of my life.

I've hated you for most of my life, but I've got to get rid of the hate. A very good friend told me that if I didn't, it would destroy me.

I think he's right.

Chapter Two

My task was simple. I was supposed to find out as much as I could about my mother. Tim had the crazy notion that if I could understand her and perhaps even learn why she had abandoned me, it would help me exorcize my personal demons.

I didn't think it would be anywhere near that simple since I had to do this alone, but I didn't have any better ideas to offer, so I agreed to come on this fool's errand.

But where was I to start? I'm a CEO, not an investigator.

Up to now I hadn't even been able to discover my mother's name.

So for lack of a better place to start, I decided to visit my last known address in Fairbanks. I told Ryan I wanted to get an early start and to bring a pair of bunny boots for me. He was waiting in the lobby when I came down at eight fifteen.

"Where would you like to go, Mr. Rush?" asked Ryan.

"The Kellner Children's Home," I said.

Ryan hesitated. "Are you sure?"

I nodded.

"Okay," he said.

I couldn't quite read his voice, but it sounded strange.

Ryan pulled out and started driving toward the home. At my request he had traded our limo for something a bit more practical—a four-wheel-drive Jeep Cherokee.

I was nine years old when I left Alaska. The last five years there were spent at the Kellner Children's Home. For all I know, that's where my mother dropped me off. The home was established in the 1950s by Gladys Kellner, a woman who had no children of her own but had enough love for hundreds. By the time I was there, she had passed away. But her legacy lived on.

It was eight thirty in the morning and still pitch dark outside. I strained to see through the darkness as Ryan rolled the Jeep up the long driveway toward the main house. Something didn't look right.

The main gate was closed, but that wasn't the problem. The problem was the bright yellow sign attached to the gate.

"Closed. No trespassing."

My heart sank.

"Wait here," I told Ryan.

I got out of the Jeep and walked up to the iron gate. It was padlocked with a heavy chain.

I squinted, trying to make out the details of the main house. It was still too dark to see much, but from this distance it looked like a bombed-out World War II relic. A few thick stone walls still stood, but the building was a blackened shell. Open holes gaped where once there were windows. A few heavy beams jutted from the ruins.

I knew it was useless to waste any more time here, but I'd come too far to be stopped at the front gate. I went back to the Jeep and climbed in.

"What happened?" I asked.

"I don't know," said Ryan. "It was already closed when I moved up here." He turned back and looked at me. "Where would you like to go now, sir?"

"Inside."

Ryan flashed me a puzzled look.

"Drive around to the back entrance."

"But, Mr. Rush . . ."

"Just do it."

Ryan backed down the driveway and pulled onto the road. About half a block farther down, we intersected with another road. "Hang a left here," I told him.

"Sir, are you sure . . ."

"Left, Ryan."

Ryan threw me another look that seemed to say, "It's your funeral," but he turned and followed the road around to the back of the property.

"There's a place back here where the older kids used to sneak out at night," I said. "Mr. King, the custodian, kept a pretty good eye on us, but there was a place where the fence line crossed right through the trunk of a willow tree. Rather than cut the tree down, they just brought the fence up to one side of the trunk and continued it on the other.

"We got pretty good at climbing the willow. It was our private exit. As far as I know, he never figured it out."

"Ummm. This is not exactly tree-climbing weather, sir."

"Let's just see what we find."

We got around to the back gate, which was just as imposing as the front. It was also padlocked with a heavy chain.

"Come on," I said. "I'll need your help."

"Mr. Rush," Ryan replied, "I don't think it's a good id—"

"Where's your sense of adventure?"

"I could get fired," he said.

"Look. If they fire you, I'll hire you as my personal driver. Will that work for you?"

He looked exasperated.

"I take care of people, Ryan. And if I take care of you, you won't regret it," I said. "Let's go."

Ryan sighed and got out of the Jeep.

We were in luck. About ten feet to the left of the gate was the place where the willow had stood. Now there was only a snow-covered stump. It looked like the tree had fallen fairly recently because most of it lay inside the fence line and the hole in the fence had been patched with a web of yellow caution tape.

The Arctic cold had made the plastic brittle, and Ryan and I had little difficulty tearing it apart. I stepped inside the fence and followed it back to the gate. "Aren't you coming?" I asked.

Ryan shook his head. "This is as far as I go, Mr. Rush. Trespassing is not in my job description."

"Okay," I said. "You can wait in the Jeep. This shouldn't take long."

The sun was peeking above the horizon as I made my way up the stone walkway toward the main house. There was a large gap where the huge oak front doors had once stood. I entered the remnants of the building that I had called home for five years of my life. Thick stone walls surrounded what had once been the building's foundation, but they were now broken and jagged, covered with a blanket of snow.

My bedroom had been on the second floor, but even if it were still there, I'd have had no way to get to it. The staircase had been completely burned away. I stood on a small patch of blackened earth inside a hollow stone shell.

If I had had any hope of finding out about my mother here, it evaporated. The main office, which had been off the first floor, was completely gone. And the building had long since been cleaned out. It wouldn't have mattered even if it hadn't been. The fire had obviously destroyed everything.

I just wish my memories could be burned away as easily as this building was.

I heard footsteps crunching on the snow behind me.

"Changed your mind, did you?" I said as I turned around.

My mouth went dry as I found myself looking down the twin barrels of a 12-gauge shotgun.

Chapter Three

Ada Rose Guthrie had a routine, and she followed it closely. Up by five every morning. Stoke the fire in the wood stove. Take Tundra out to do his business. Then off to Merv's for breakfast.

Since Ada walked nearly everywhere she went, it was much easier to follow her routine during the warm summer months. Once winter kicked in, she had to stay house-bound most of the time. A few of the local churches would drive her around if she asked. But Ada didn't have a phone.

Of course, there was bus service out her way. She could hop on the Gray Line and go anywhere she needed to, but she didn't like taking the bus. It didn't fit her schedule, didn't fit her timing. And there were too many people. Too many.

So mostly she walked.

Problem was, if she didn't go out to Merv's, she didn't get breakfast. That meant she had to wait for the Meals on Wheels delivery, and sometimes that didn't get there until late in the afternoon.

So even in the winter, she would venture out if it was warm enough.

It was only about seventeen below this morning, and there wasn't much wind. So today she would have breakfast. She pulled on her old worn Carhartts, a couple pairs of socks, bunny boots, fur-lined mittens, a sweater, a ski mask, and a scarf, and topped it all off with a hooded parka, then started the half-mile walk to Merv's.

Some days, if she was lucky, someone would stop and give her a ride.

She hadn't been lucky today, but it didn't matter now. The bright lights around Big Merv's Diner were an inviting sight. Kind of like an oasis in a desert.

Ada had never been in a desert—she had never been out of Alaska—but she kind of figured this is what walking through a desert would be like.

Except for the cold, of course.

A little bell over the door tinkled as Ada pushed it open and went inside. The blast of warm air felt as refreshing as a hot bubble bath at the end of a long day.

A handful of men were sitting at the counter, drinking coffee and talking to one of the waitresses. They glanced over her way and waved.

Ada nodded and shuffled over to her regular table, near the wood stove.

She took off her parka, scarf, mittens, and ski mask and laid them neatly over the chair beside her. The man at the table next to hers was reading the *Daily News-Miner*.

Ada glowered at him and muttered. She didn't usually have to wait to read the paper. It was part of her routine. Didn't he know that?

A meaty hand set down a heavy mug in front of her.

"How's my favorite lady in the whole world?" a deep, cheerful voice crooned as another large hand poured coffee into the cup.

"Okay," Ada said.

She didn't look up at him. Didn't need to. She knew Merv Junior's voice.

"Will it be the usual today?"

Ada nodded and then looked over at the man with the newspaper.

Merv wiped his hands on the apron covering his large belly. He bent down close. "Yeah, I know. I'm sorry," he whispered. "He'll be done soon."

Ada noticed that the man's plate was only half empty. Besides that, Merv had just poured him a fresh cup of coffee too.

She certainly hoped that he would be done soon. She didn't have all day.

"I'll be back in a few minutes with your breakfast, doll."

Ada blushed. Merv always called her that. But she didn't believe she really deserved it. She didn't feel like someone's doll. And she knew she certainly did not look like she could be someone's doll.

The man at the next table rattled the newspaper and folded it. Then he waved at Merv. "Check, please." He took a long sip of coffee and wiped his face with the red cloth napkin. Merv always used red cloth napkins. Ada had no idea why.

A few minutes later Merv set down a plate in front of Ada: two eggs over easy, yokes not broken; hash browns; two sausage links. It was steaming hot, but she couldn't eat yet.

Merv refilled her coffee and gave the man at the next table his check.

"Thanks," the man said. He got up to go over to the checkout counter. He didn't look Ada's way, and she didn't look his way either. Her eye was on the newspaper.

Finally she leaned over and pulled it toward her.

Now she could eat.

The newspaper sat untouched until she finished eating. The regular customers knew that she had first claim on the paper, and it was usually waiting at her table when she came in. Problem was, she couldn't read most of it. The print was too small, and she had no glasses. But she still liked to read the headlines. They were big enough.

When she opened the paper, a larger-than-usual head-line caught her eye.

For a few seconds she thought that her heart might stop.

She couldn't believe it, but there it was, big as life. She squinted and tried to hold the paper close to her eyes so she could read the smaller print, but it was no good. She had to get home. Right away.

Ada looked over at Merv. He was busy with another

customer. She quickly folded the front page into a small package and put it in her sweater pocket. Then she bundled up for the half-mile walk home.

"Leaving already, doll?" Merv called from behind the counter.

Ada looked down and nodded.

"Need a ride?"

She shook her head.

"Okay. See you tomorrow, if it's not too cold," Merv called after her.

Ada pulled open the door. The little bell tinkled again, and she felt the blast of cold as she walked out into the subzero air.

───

Ada threw some more wood into the stove and closed the iron door. She pulled her rocker as close to the stove as she could, and Tundra plopped down at her feet. When the temperature outside is seventeen below, even a husky grabs warmth wherever he can get it.

Ada knew that Merv wouldn't mind that she had taken part of the paper. This wasn't the first time she had done it. But she did it only on certain days.

Today was one of those days.

She never told Merv why she took the papers, and he never asked. But she always watched for special news items. Today the headline on the front page was as good as it got. She set her coffee down and unfolded the newspaper. She read the headline again, just to be sure it was really true.

"Jonathan 'Gold' Rush Visits Fairbanks."

Ada picked up a large magnifying glass from her nearby coffee table and moved the glass over the tiny print.

"By Erica Bingham."

The article was not long:

JONATHON "GOLD" RUSH VISITS FAIRBANKS

by Erica Bingham

Fairbanks native Jonathan "Gold" Rush flew into town yesterday afternoon, reportedly to scout locations for a branch office of Advanced Data Systems.

Jonathan Rush, nicknamed "Gold" because of his apparent ability to turn every business he touches into a profitable enterprise, has led a troubled life over the last few years. The breakup of his third marriage two years ago was followed by an accidental overdose of prescription painkillers last August. There has been speculation in the media that Rush's overdose was not accidental, but that has never been confirmed.

Some sources are saying that Rush, who is staying at the Chena Resort, wants to get away from the hectic lifestyle of Miami and return to a quieter life here in Fairbanks.

Local leaders are excited about the possibilities. If ADS opens a branch office, it could bring hundreds of new jobs to the community.

Mr. Rush refused to comment on the truth of the rumors.■

Ada sat there, stunned. She couldn't believe what she'd just read.

Jonathan Rush might be coming back to Fairbanks to live.

With trembling hands, Ada clipped the article from the front page. She opened a thick, worn scrapbook, found an empty page, and taped the article to it.

Chapter Four

I wouldn't make any sudden moves if I was you," a gruff voice growled.

I squinted, trying to make out the face of the person behind the gun. But he was shining a flashlight in my eyes and I couldn't see anything else.

I raised my hands. "I'm sorry. I didn't mean to trespass."

"Course you did," the man said. "Ain't no other way you'd get in here than by trespassing."

"Well, you've got me there," I said. "Truth is, I used to live here, and I couldn't resist coming in for a peek at the old place. Or what is left of it."

"Name?"

"Jonathan Rush."

"Gold Rush?" There was a note of wonder in his voice.

"I hate that nickname, but yes. That's me."

He lowered his flashlight and pointed the barrels of the shotgun toward the ground.

I blinked a few times, trying to bring my eyes back into focus. The man who stood before me was short and stocky, with a long white beard and beat-up horn-rimmed glasses. I hadn't seen his face in decades, but I'd never forget him.

"Mr. King?" I said. "You're still here?"

He smiled a broad and nearly toothless smile. "Yep. Still lookin' after the old place."

"You live here?"

Silas King nodded. "Caretaker's cabin is the only building that didn't burn."

"Mr. King," I said, "I hate to impose on you, but would you have time to answer a few questions?"

He nodded. "Let's go up to my cabin and get out of the cold."

⁜

The caretaker's cabin was comfortable, if sparsely furnished. He brought me a steaming cup of coffee as we sat at his kitchen table.

"Why do they keep you on here, now that the school is closed?" I asked.

"Mostly to keep out trespassers and vandals—like you." He winked. "The Kellner Foundation closed down the school after the fire, but there are still a lot of lawsuits going on. They'll probably keep me here till all is said and done. After that, who knows?"

"What happened?" I asked.

"'Twas in the summer of 2002. A boy, about thirteen as I recall. They punished him for somethin'. I don't remember what. Didn't take it well. During the night, he snuck out to the equipment shed and got some gasoline. Torched every build-ing on the property except this one. He put the gas can out here by my door, then ran and tried to make it look like he was helpin' rescue people." Mr. King shook his head and looked out the window. "At first, they thought I done it. Caused me a world of trouble." His voice got quiet. "Three children and a house-mother died. They closed the place down not long after. Ain't been open since."

We sat there for a few minutes in silence, listening to the old structure creaking against the cold air.

Mr. King finally broke the silence. "What did you want to ask me?"

"I know it's a long shot, but did any of the records survive the fire?"

He shook his head. "Nope. Main building was a total loss. Why?"

"I'm trying to find out something about the woman who left me here. But if the records are gone . . ."

"When did she leave you?"

"I was four."

"And you're, what, forty now?"

"Thirty-five. My birthday is later in the year."

"So she'd have dropped you off about nineteen seventy-nine." Mr. King sat, silent and thoughtful, stroking his beard. "I didn't start here till eighty. And not many people who worked at the home are still around. There's one lady you might try, if you can find her. Used to be a cook."

"What's her name?"

Mr. King shook his head. "Don't remember. She left

before I got here, but she still lives in Fairbanks. Used to cook at the Baptist church on Wednesday nights, but I don't know if she still does. You might try there."

Ryan was waiting in the Jeep with the engine running when I finally left Mr. King's cabin.

"Where to now?" he asked.

I looked at my watch. I was supposed to check in with Tim before ten o'clock. "Let's go back to the hotel. I need to make some phone calls before we do anything else."

Ryan nodded and pulled back out onto the street.

It was almost nine thirty, and the sun was hovering above the horizon. It wouldn't get much higher in the sky today. The snow-covered landscape was shrouded in the bluish-gray light of early morning. As we drove through Fairbanks, I began to wonder whether I was going to accomplish anything worthwhile on this trip or whether it was going to be one huge exercise in frustration. Fairbanks wasn't a huge city. But still, trying to find one person in a city of about thirty-five thousand was no small task, especially when you didn't have a name or address.

And worse than that, it could all be for nothing. Even if I found this person, there was no guarantee that she knew anything about my mother.

Not that I really cared. If it weren't for Tim, I wouldn't have come here in the first place.

After we got back to the hotel, I gave Ryan the rest of the day off. When it came right down to it, I just didn't feel like searching for this mystery lady. I wanted to go to bed, pull the covers over my head, and sleep.

As soon as I got in my room, I turned my cell phone on.

It started ringing almost before my thumb left the power button.

"Hi, Tim," I said.

"So how's it going?" His voice was bright and chipper.

"It's going."

"Did you write the letter?"

"I started it."

"Okay," he said. "I'll take that. How far did you get?"

"I got to the part where if I didn't get rid of the hate, it would destroy me."

"Excellent," Tim replied. "So how're you doing with that?"

I kicked off my bunny boots and sat down on the bed. "I'm trying not to think about it."

"Have you learned anything about your mother yet?"

"Only that nobody seems to know anything about her. Not even her name."

"Keep trying," Tim said. "I don't want you leaving there until you know something about her."

"I suppose you'll take care of running my business while I'm gone."

"Don't go sarcastic on me," Tim said. "You may be a control freak, but you've trained your people well. That operation can run on autopilot, and you know it."

"Tim, look—"

"No excuses, my friend. You're not leaving there until you've tried to understand this woman."

I disconnected. Then I swore and threw the BlackBerry across the room, sending it ricocheting off a painting and landing behind a leather recliner. I didn't care if I broke it. Actually, I hoped that I did. I hadn't told Tim what hotel I'd be staying at, and if my phone broke, I wouldn't have to talk to him anymore.

The BlackBerry started to chirp.

I sighed. Just my luck.

I let it chirp and went downstairs to get some breakfast.

Peak breakfast time was long past, so there weren't many customers in the restaurant. I was happy for that. The local paper had printed a photo of me on the front page, along with the headline "Jonathan 'Gold' Rush Visits Fairbanks." The last thing I wanted was a crowd of eager hometowners wanting autographs or, worse, jobs. As far as I knew, word hadn't yet gotten out about where I was staying unless, of course, that reporter had disclosed my whereabouts in her article.

I gave the server my order and opened the copy of *USA Today* that I'd found outside my door this morning. I wasn't interested in catching up on the local Fairbanks news, particularly since I was the lead story.

I was halfway through the business section when someone brought me a cup of coffee. That wouldn't have been unusual in itself, but she also sat down across the table from me.

"Uhhh, what are you doing?" I asked.

28

"Bringing you coffee. You ordered coffee, didn't you?"

"I did, but I didn't realize that the staff would sit with me while I drank it. Do you charge extra for this service, or am I just expected to leave a bigger tip?"

"I don't work here," she said.

"That much, I'd figured out. Now, who are you?"

"You really don't remember me?"

I was about to say no when it flooded back: young, eager woman reporter who wouldn't take no for an answer. "The airport."

"Correct," she said. "Erica Bingham." She offered her hand.

I didn't take it.

"Ms. Bingham, are you into self-punishment?"

She looked puzzled.

"I figure you must be. Otherwise, you wouldn't be harassing me again. I thought I made myself clear at the airport. I'm here on personal business, and I don't want to be disturbed. I especially don't want to do any interviews. Now, I see you already managed to get a front-page article out of our little encounter yesterday. That's all you're going to get from me. So if I were you, I'd be happy and leave."

Erica stared at me a few seconds. She looked thoughtful, almost as if she were sizing me up for her next attack. Finally, she spoke. "What will it take for me to get an interview?"

I'd been a public figure long enough to have dealt with all kinds of reporters. Some were stubborn. Others were arrogant. Some tried to catch you saying or doing something they could exploit. A few tried whatever tricks they could manage, just to get you to talk to them. None of them had anything on this young lady where persistence was concerned.

"Why do you do this to yourself?" I asked her.

"What?"

"Beat your head against the wall, hoping I'll change my mind."

Erica leaned back in her chair and smiled. "Because I'm very good at what I do. If there's a story out there, I'm going to get it."

"Which begs the question," I said. "If you're so good, why are you here in Fairbanks? This isn't exactly a hotbed for hard news."

She shrugged and looked away. "I have my reasons."

I'd seen that uncomfortable look in other people, and I knew I had her. "You tell me why you're in Fairbanks, and I'll tell you why I'm here," I said.

Erica stood up. "Your coffee's getting cold," she said. Then she turned and walked out of the restaurant.

By the time I'd finished my breakfast, it was past noon. Ryan wouldn't be back until tomorrow morning, and I didn't have any intention of going out on my own. I've always been stubborn that way. When someone tries to push me into doing something I don't want to do, I dig in my heels and find creative ways to procrastinate.

Tim calls it passive aggression; I like calling it stubborn

resistance. Finding ways to control the situation. Showing that I am more powerful.

Whatever.

As I left the restaurant, I noticed that the hotel had a nicely equipped exercise room. I am not a health freak by any means, and I don't spend a lot of time exercising. But since the alternative was either to hunt for information about my mother or write her a letter she would never read, exercise sounded pretty good. Plus, I wanted to be alone, and hotel exercise rooms are notoriously deserted.

I went up to my room and changed into my sweats. My BlackBerry was still under the recliner, and I was more than happy to leave it there. Then I went back down to the exercise room and got on one of the ellipticals.

I had worked up a good sweat when Erica Bingham came through the door.

"Deal," she said.

I was nonplussed. "Deal?"

"I'm agreeing to your terms. I'll tell you why I'm here in Fairbanks."

The machine kept pumping my legs and arms. "Wait a minute now," I said. "I didn't—"

She pulled out a little notebook. "You said, and I quote, 'You tell me why you're in Fairbanks, and I'll tell you why I'm here.'"

I punched the stop button and climbed off the machine. "Throw me a towel," I said.

Erica went over to the rack and threw me a thick hand towel. I wiped my face and put it over my shoulder.

"So do we have a deal?" she said.

I hated to admit it, but she had me this time, whether she knew it or not. I don't break promises. Of course, I'd never have made this one if I thought she was going to take me up on it.

"I guess we have a deal, but I need to take a shower first."

"In the restaurant in about a half hour?" she said.

"That'll be fine. But you're buying," I told her.

She grinned and tossed her curly hair out of her eyes. "I can handle that," she said as she left the room.

I smiled and shook my head as I watched her go. Surprisingly, I was kind of looking forward to talking to her.

She just might make the short list of reporters that I liked.

Chapter Five

Ada Guthrie still couldn't quite believe it. Jonathan Rush was coming back to Fairbanks to live. That's what the newspaper said. A flood of conflicting emotions swept through her: joy, fear, excitement, guilt.

Mostly guilt.

She drew a pot of water from a five-gallon jug and put it on the stove to boil. Dry cabin living in Alaska could be primitive, but even if she could have afforded a better place, she'd have it no other way. It wasn't so much that she liked her life. She'd occasionally toyed with the idea of moving to a better location. A place with running water and an indoor toilet definitely appealed to her, particularly as she got older.

She lived a hard life, and with each passing year it got more difficult to maintain her independence as a struggling artist.

It would definitely be easier to move into a complex. Maybe a retirement home.

But there were reasons she stayed where she was.

Partly it was because she didn't like to be around people that much. If she went to an apartment complex, even a low-rent one, she'd have to be around people. Have to social-ize. Ada liked to keep to herself, liked her privacy. She'd been that way for too many years to change now.

But that wasn't the main reason Ada kept to herself. To be honest, she didn't feel she had a right to be around people.

Not after all the things she had done.

She guessed that was the main reason she stayed on the outskirts of Fairbanks in an old cabin that probably should have been torn down years ago.

Ada poured a cup of coffee and sat down at her kitchen table as she waited for the wash water to boil. She ran her fingers over the cover of her scrapbook and hummed the tune to her favorite hymn.

Ada closed her eyes, and as she hummed, she thought back to when Jonathan was a little boy. He was so full of life. So full of love.

Sometimes she imagined what it would be like to meet Jonathan now, to talk to him. She'd watched him from afar for so many years, kept track of everything he did. What would it be like to sit down and visit, to learn about all the wonderful things he'd accomplished?

She was so proud of him. As proud as any mother ever could be.

But she realized that she would never talk to him or meet him. That could never be.

Jonathan Rush knew nothing about her, and she wanted it that way.

The teapot on the stove began to whistle, and Ada changed the pitch of her humming to bring it in tune. She poured the water into a basin and got ready to wash the dirty dishes that had piled up over the last few days.

She continued to hum as she plopped the dishes into the basin and poured a little soap over them. Soon Ada was softly singing:

> There's a wideness in God's mercy
> Like the wideness of the sea;
> There's a kindness in his justice,
> Which is more than liberty.
> There is welcome for the sinner,
> And more graces for the good;
> There is mercy with the Savior;
> There is healing in his blood.

Chapter Six

Erica had already ordered the coffee and had it waiting for me when I came down from my room.

I pulled up a chair and took a sip from the cup.

"You first," I said. "Why is a hotshot investigative reporter hanging out in Fairbanks, Alaska? I don't know much about the newspaper business, but I'm fairly certain this isn't the kind of place you want to go for career advancement."

She took a deep breath and looked down into her cup.

"Not much to tell, really," she said. "I grew up here, and my parents still live here. After I got my degree in journalism, I moved to Seattle and went to work at the *Post-Intelligencer*. It didn't work out so well, and I came home. End of story."

I raised an eyebrow. "Ms. Bingham, you're going to have to do a lot better than that if you expect me to tell you anything."

A shadow of pain crossed her face. She continued in halting sentences.

"I met a guy there . . . at the newspaper. We fell in love." She held up her left hand and showed me the diamond engagement ring she wore. "Planned to be married. Even set the date. He was everything I'd ever wanted in a man."

"And he cheated on you? Left you?"

She shook her head.

"He . . . umm . . . he . . ." She was blinking back tears now. "There was a story he was working on and . . ." She took her spoon and started stirring her coffee. "It was about a small-time crime boss." She took a deep breath and let it out with a shudder.

"It's okay," I said. "You don't have to tell me anymore."

"No," she said. "I want to finish." She sipped some coffee and continued. "He called me one Friday night and told me that he had a great lead. He was going to break the story wide open. That was the last I ever heard from him. They found his body a few days later."

"I'm sorry," I said.

"I came home to stay with my parents for a few weeks. Get over things." She looked up at me and shrugged. "I just never went back." She took a napkin and dabbed at her eyes. "It's not perfect up here by any means," she said. "But I guess I'd had enough of big-city living. Big-city dying. So I took a job at the *Miner* and have been here ever since. We don't have a lot of big news, but that's okay. And" —her lips curled up in a grin— "that's why whenever we do get big news, like a visit from the CEO of a Fortune 500 company who also happens to be a hometown boy, we kind of get excited."

I laughed. "I guess that means it's my turn."

"You got it," she said.

"How much of my story do you know? I don't want to waste a lot of time giving you my life history."

"Well, let's see," she said. "I know you were born in

Fairbanks and lived at the Kellner Home till you were nine. A family named Rush adopted you and took you to live in the lower forty-eight. You didn't particularly stand out in school, except for your ability in math and computer science. You went to MIT and ended up starting a computer company that's running a close third behind Microsoft and Apple." She grinned. "How's that?"

"Pretty good," I said.

"So what brings you to Fairbanks, Mr. Rush? Is it true that you're planning on moving your company's offices up here?"

I shook my head. "Sorry. Nothing so dramatic."

She looked disappointed. "So the tabloids are right? You're here because of what's happened over the last couple of years?"

"Sort of," I said. "Look, I was telling you the truth when I said that I'm here on some personal business. If I tell you what it is, I'd appreciate it if it could be off the record."

She nodded. "Okay. I can live with that."

"I'm here in search of my roots, you might say. I don't remember my mother, but I do remember that she abandoned me when I was four."

"When she left you at the Kellner Home?"

I nodded.

"I've never gotten over it. It's been eating me alive most of my life. For a long time I kept my feelings buried and just focused on my work. But over the last few years, I've gotten angrier and angrier. It's affecting my relationships, my health, even my business."

I looked out the window. It was only about three fifteen, but the shadows outside were lengthening. The sun would soon go down.

"So what are you hoping to accomplish here?"

"I'm not hoping to accomplish anything. My pastor, on the other hand, seems to think I will benefit by learning about my mother. Who she is. Why she abandoned me. I promised him that I'd come up here and see what I could find out."

"Have you had any luck?"

"Not so far. I saw what was left of the Kellner Home this morning and talked to the caretaker, but he doesn't know anything. He says there's a lady in town who used to be a cook out there, and she might know something. But he didn't know her name. He said she cooked at the Baptist church on Wednesday nights, but wasn't even sure that she was still doing that."

"Have you checked any other sources?"

I drained my coffee cup. "Don't know what to check. Like I told him, I'm a software developer, not an investigator."

Erica's blue eyes brightened. "I might be able to help you with that."

I raised my eyebrows. "Off the record?"

She smiled. "Off the record. No story."

I held out my hand.

She took it.

"Deal," we both said.

Chapter Seven

Ada never planned on being a single mother. Never planned on being single at all. Like every other girl her age, she'd had dreams that the right young man would come along; then they would get married and live happily ever after.

Funny how life doesn't work out the way you plan it.

A young man had come along. Jared Cooper was his name. He was everything she had ever imagined he would be. Tall. Handsome. Muscular. He came up to Fairbanks to work on the pipeline, and one afternoon he walked into Merv's where she was working as a waitress. The first time he walked through the door, she knew her dream man had come into her life.

She didn't really know how she knew, but she did.

He had thick black hair and intense blue eyes. Ada had never met someone who had black hair and blue eyes. When he looked at her, it was like he was looking into her soul. He flirted with her and she flirted back. It wasn't too long before they were an item. They had a whirlwind romance, maybe not the kind you read about in a glitzy romance novel, but a romance nonetheless.

Jared was a roughneck at the pipeline, and he often was away from Fairbanks for weeks at a time. Ada didn't mind. She treasured every minute they were able to spend together.

It was the best year of her life.

One of her favorite memories was of a warm early summer afternoon when Jared had some time off. He came over to her cabin, and they sat out back with binoculars, watching a cow moose walking with her calf by the tree line in the distance.

Jared was fascinated by the moose and wanted to get closer, to get a better view, but Ada told him they couldn't. No matter how docile moose appeared, they were dangerous animals. Ada knew hunters who had told her they preferred facing a grizzly bear to facing an angry moose any day. Jared was not convinced, and he crossed the green field to see the moose on his own. It took out after him and gave him the chase of his life.

Jared didn't get hurt, but he was so scared, his face looked like someone had coated it with whitewash. Ada laughed so hard her sides hurt. Once Jared calmed down, he laughed too. And he never went to meet a moose up close again.

Jared loved Alaska, and Ada was certain that when his work on the pipeline was finished, he would decide to stay with her. They could live in her cabin. It wasn't much, but it was the only thing she owned. They would have a good life together.

But it hadn't worked out that way.

One day, Jared just failed to show up. She waited for him, thinking through possible reasons he might be late. But he never came.

She worried about him for weeks. The pipeline was a

dangerous job, and he would not be the first man to lose his life working on it. But finally a letter arrived at the restaurant, addressed to her.

She was working the lunch shift when it came, and she didn't have time to read it then. When she did, she wished she hadn't. Wished the letter had never come. Wished he had just left her thinking he was dead.

The letter did not say much. Only that Jared would miss her, but that his work was done now, and he had to return to Texas.

Ada felt as though someone had taken a butcher knife and plunged it into her heart. How stupid and blind had she been?

She spent the rest of the day in a fog. She stayed at the restaurant. Went through the motions. Then went back to her cabin and cried herself to sleep. For a time, she thought about killing herself. What did she have to live for, anyway?

But she didn't.

She couldn't.

Ada had no problem with the idea of taking her own life. As far as she was concerned, her main reason for living had walked out on her.

But she had more than one life to think about now.

Ada wondered whether there was some way she could see Jonathan.

Not talk to him. Not meet him.

Just see him.

It was a crazy idea, she knew, but she couldn't get it out of her head. It wouldn't be easy, and it had to be secret. He could never know who she was or that she was even watching him.

But how would she be able to do it?

Ada flipped her scrapbook open to the page where she'd taped today's *News-Miner* article. The article had mentioned where Jonathan was staying. Ada was sure of it. She took out her magnifying glass and scanned the clipped piece of newsprint till she found what she was looking for. Jonathan was staying at the Chena Resort.

She went over to the old chest of drawers, where she kept most of her belongings, and pulled out a pint-sized mason jar filled with coins and bills. She didn't have much in there, probably not more than twenty dollars.

Ada dumped the change onto her kitchen table and counted out three dollar bills and eight quarters. She didn't think she would need much. Just enough for bus fare to the resort. And enough to buy a cup of coffee. Five dollars should do it.

Jonathan had to eat sooner or later.

If she had to, she would just sit there and drink coffee until he showed up.

Chapter Eight

Had I made a deal with the devil? I hoped not. I spent most
of my life—indeed, I had developed a reputation for—dodg-
ing the media. It felt strange to be working with a reporter. But
if Erica Bingham could help me end this business quickly and
get back to Miami, it would be worth it.

When I got back to my room, I found several short and
sweet text messages from Tim.

"How r u doing?"

"R u there?"

"Helloooooo?"

I sighed. Tim was like a hound dog on a scent. He
wouldn't let it go until he heard from me. In fact, unless I
missed my guess, a voice mail or two waited for me.

I checked, and sure enough, Tim had left three.

"Hi, Jon. Just checking in to see how things are coming
along. You're not avoiding me, are you?"

Tim's voice was playful, but I knew he was serious. If I
didn't call him soon, he would just keep nagging me. The
problem was, I had to be careful about what I said to him. I
didn't want to tip him off to the fact that I was bending the

rules a bit. He had told me I needed to search for information about my mother alone. I couldn't hire someone else to do it for me.

But he meant hiring a private investigator to do all the work for me. He didn't say anything about having someone help me. Still, I wasn't taking any chances.

I speed-dialed Tim's number and waited for him to pick up.

"I was beginning to wonder if I'd ever hear from you," Tim said.

"Sorry," I replied. "I've been busy."

"Are you sure that's all it is?"

"What else do you think I've been doing?" I said, a little irritation creeping into my voice. "I've been doing exactly what you told me to do, trying to learn as much as I can about my mother so I can finish this fool's errand and get back to Miami."

"I thought you liked Fairbanks," Tim said.

"I do. In the summer."

Tim laughed. "The cold weather is a good motivator, then. You'll work harder just so you can get out of there."

"Or it could just keep me in my room, not getting anything done."

"Did you finish the letter to your mother?"

"I still don't see the point of it, but yes, I finished it."

"Would you read it to me?"

My throat felt like it was going to close up on me. "Right now?"

"Uh-huh," Tim said.

"Tim," I said, "I don't think I can do that. Not yet."

"Jon, you're how old?"

"Thirty-five. Why?"

"And you were how old when your mother abandoned you?"

"Four."

"So for the last thirty-one years you've been carrying around this extra baggage. What was it you told me when we first talked?"

I sighed. "I've spent half my life hating myself and the other half hating her."

"Six months ago you tried to kill yourself. Do you remember what you wrote on your suicide note?"

My voice thickened. "Life hurts too much."

"You have everything a person could ever want. Why did you say life hurts?"

I couldn't answer. Not without falling apart right there over the phone.

"Jon? Are you there?"

I barely managed to croak out a reply. "I'm here."

"My friend, you've been bottling up that pain and anger for thirty-one years. You're successful for a little while, but sooner or later the pressure gets too great. When that happens, the cork blows off that bottle, and that anger spews out like acid, burning you and everyone you come in contact with."

I nodded. "I know."

"You don't have to read me the letter to your mother. I just want you to understand there's a point to everything I'm asking you to do. No matter what you think, I didn't send you up there on a fool's errand. Your life may well depend on what you learn. Because if you don't deal with your feelings toward this woman, find some way to get them out and resolve them, that acid you're bottling up is eventually going to explode. And the next time it does, it's going to destroy you. It's time to deal with those feelings, Jon."

"Yeah, I know," I said, and I disconnected.

I told Erica that I'd meet her at 5:30 p.m. in the resort's atrium. We'd agreed that the first place to continue the search for information about my mother was at the Fellowship Baptist Church's Wednesday evening supper. We hoped we could find the mystery cook Silas King had told me about this morning.

When I got down to the atrium at 5:25, she was waiting for me.

I glanced at my watch and smiled. "Prompt. I like that."

"I was about to say the same thing," she replied. "Are you ready?"

I pulled the hood of my parka onto my head and motioned toward the door. "Lead on."

I was surprised when Erica led me out into the parking lot and we stopped in front of a late-model Toyota Corolla.

"I thought everybody up here had four-wheel drive," I said.

Erica laughed as we got in. "It's not that I wouldn't love to have a big four-by-four SUV," she said. "But this is what I can afford. Besides, if you've got front-wheel drive and a good set of snow tires, you'd be surprised how well you can do. But I have to admit that the low clearance can be a problem until the snow plows get the roads into manageable shape."

"How far away is the church?" I asked.

"Just a few miles," she said. "It won't take long to get there."

We rolled through downtown Fairbanks on Airport Way. A display in front of one of the local banks showed the current temperature to be about twenty below.

"What's the biggest challenge nowadays, living up here?" I asked.

Erica smiled and shook her head. "You probably would get a different answer from every person you asked. For me, it's this time of year. I love spring and summer, but the winters get to me."

"You don't like the cold?"

She shook her head. "It's not the cold. It's the long nights. It can get pretty depressing when you have only a few hours of actual sunlight each day. And even then the sun doesn't get very high in the sky. A lot of people up here—me included—struggle with SAD, seasonal affective disorder. But as long as I sit in front of a light therapy lamp for a half hour or so a day, I'm good."

"Ever think of leaving here for a sunnier climate?" I asked.

"Did you have any place in mind?"

"Oh, I don't know," I said. "Miami's very nice this time of year. They've got some great newspapers. And you'd never have to worry about SAD again."

Erica shook her head. "This place kind of grows on you. It gets in your blood. Do you know what I mean? It's hard to explain, but every now and then I'll think about leaving here. Then I'll be out some night and see the aurora. After all these years I'm still awestruck every time I see it. It's like God has a gigantic set of watercolors and he's splashing green and red paint across the sky."

"That's one of the few things I can remember about living here," I said. "It does make an impression, doesn't it?"

She nodded. "And it probably sounds kind of silly to someone as busy as you are, but life moves at a slower pace here. And I can't say enough about the people. They're great."

"I think you missed your calling," I said. "You should be writing travel brochures. Keep talking and I might go ahead and move my offices up here after all."

Erica slowed down and signaled a left turn.

"Here we are," she said.

I don't know what I expected Fellowship Baptist Church to look like, but I don't think any mental picture I could have thought up would have been remotely close to the reality. I'm a member of one of Miami's megachurches. We have a membership of twenty-three thousand people, meeting on three campuses. Our facilities are technological, not to mention architectural, wonders.

In contrast, Fellowship Baptist Church could best be described as utilitarian. It was a concrete block structure that looked like it could pass for a warehouse. There was a little steeple, if you could call it that, on the front. A cross made out of a couple pieces of one-by-two had been attached to the top of the little steeple.

There were about fifteen cars in the parking lot, and the aroma coming from the building was heavenly.

"I don't know what they're serving for supper," I said, "but I hope they don't mind sharing."

Erica laughed as we walked toward the door. "That's what this meal is all about."

Although the church building looked like a warehouse on the outside, it felt like a family room once we stepped inside. Thirty or forty people were seated at long tables, talking, laughing, and having a good time. A few of them looked in our direction as we entered the building, but most just kept visiting with one another. They looked like they were dressed for work rather than church.

A short, balding man on the other side of the room spotted us and came over to greet us. His face had a lined, weathered look, as if he'd spent many days out in the harsh weather and wind. Yet kindness and warmth radiated from him.

"Welcome," he said. "I'm Ben Morgan. I'm the pastor here. We're so glad you've come to be with us tonight. Come on over and have some stew," he said, motioning us toward the tables.

"That would be great," I said. "But before we eat, I was wondering if we could talk to your cook."

Ben looked up at me proudly. "You're looking at him."

By the time I made it through two bowls of moose stew, I managed to bring Ben up to date on why Erica and I were there. I told him who I was and described my trip out to the Kellner Home that morning. I explained that Silas King had directed us to his church, telling us that the lady who cooked for the Wednesday night suppers might be able to give me some information about my mother.

"Son, I'd like to help you, but I'm afraid I can't," he said. "I know who you're talking about, but she passed away three years ago. That's why I do the cooking now, although everyone around here will tell you they prefer her cooking over mine any day. Can't say as I blame them, either. She cooked my meals for more than forty years, and I've never had better."

"She was your wife?" Erica broke in.

Ben nodded. "She passed just shy of our forty-fifth anniversary."

"If there's any way you can help us, anything you can tell us about my mother, I'd appreciate it. Right now, we don't even have a name."

I heard metal chairs scraping the floor and turned around to see what was happening. The entire group had begun to clear the tables. One man placed a small wooden podium on the far side of the room, while several others carried the folding chairs and arranged them in front of it.

Ben looked troubled, as if he were weighing a difficult decision.

"I don't know how much help I'll be," Ben said as he

stood up. "But I'll be happy to tell you what little I know after church is over."

<hr />

After the service Pastor Morgan invited us to the parsonage, right behind the church. The little house was every bit as plain and utilitarian as the church building. However, the hand of Ben's late wife was evident even though she had been gone for three years. The place was comfortable and warmly decorated.

And it had indoor plumbing. I didn't know what the church paid Ben, but I was glad to see that the pastor at least didn't have to live in a dry cabin.

Ben brought a tray with three mugs of coffee into the living room and set it down on the coffee table. He took his mug and moved back into a well-worn recliner.

"So what else can I tell you?" he asked.

"Well, as I told you earlier, I'm trying to find out anything I can about my mother. She aband—left—me at the Kellner Home when I was four years old. I stayed there till I was nine. When my parents adopted me, they took me to live in Miami, and I've been there ever since."

I took a sip from my mug and almost choked. I'd had strong coffee before, but you could have sealed roofs with this stuff. I wondered whether Ben's wife made the coffee at home as well as cooked.

Erica's face twitched ever so slightly when she took her first sip. Then she quietly set the mug down and added a generous amount of cream and sugar to the mix.

I cleared my throat, trying to find my voice again. "I have no information at all about my mother. I don't even know her name. Your wife worked at the home when I was brought there. I was hoping that she might know something about my mother."

"Did she tell you anything at all?" Erica asked.

Ben looked slightly uncomfortable. He rubbed his face as if he were checking to see whether he needed a shave. "Well, Martha wasn't supposed to carry any information out of there. It would have cost her her job if she had."

"I understand that," I said. "But any information you have will help. Right now, we've got nothing."

He looked over at Erica.

"You said you're a reporter for the *Miner?*" he asked. "I wouldn't want anything negative about my wife to get into the paper. She was only trying to help."

Erica raised her eyebrows and shot me a quick look.

"None of this will be in the paper," she said. "I promise."

"She's just trying to help me," I added. "I'm not very good at investigating things."

Ben nodded and stood up. "Okay," he said. "I've got to get something."

As Pastor Morgan left the room, I began to wonder what he was so concerned about. What could he possibly tell me that would reflect negatively on his wife or her memory?

I wasn't sure I wanted to know the answer to that question.

Chapter Nine

It was nine o'clock sharp: time for Ada Guthrie to go to bed.

She climbed into her single bed and pulled the covers up to her chin. Her little cabin got cold at night, even with the heat from the wood stove. Of course, if she wasn't so stingy with the wood, she could keep it warmer. But wood was expensive, and she didn't want to use it up any faster than she needed to. It didn't matter how cold it got outside anyway. Ada knew she would be quite comfortable.

Long ago she had learned to dress for inside cold, the same way she dressed for outside cold: layers. Ada wore flannel pajamas over long underwear and put a sweat suit over all of that. Her bed had flannel sheets, two patchwork quilts she had made, and a thick down comforter on top.

Then Tundra usually hopped onto the bed after she was in it. The big husky added plenty of warmth of his own.

Ada lay there in her bed, reviewing her plans for the next day.

She would get up at her usual time, five o'clock, and do her chores early. By seven she would be ready for breakfast, but this time she would have to skip her daily trip to Big

Merv's for her free breakfast. Instead, she would head out to the bus stop and ride over to Chena Resort.

Ada couldn't afford to buy breakfast at the resort, so she would have to settle for coffee. Even that would be expensive. She was pretty sure, though, that the five dollars she had set out would be enough.

After that, all she had to do was to wait. She hoped that she wouldn't have to wait very long. Sooner or later the restaurant management would realize that she wasn't going to buy anything other than coffee. Then they would ask her to leave.

If that happened, she guessed she would have to try again another day.

But she only had so much cash and wouldn't be able to do this very many times.

She just had to see Jonathan.

It was true that she had "seen" him many times over the years, if you counted newspaper and magazine articles. And although she didn't have a television, she had occasionally seen him on the TV news when she was at Big Merv's.

It was hard to believe that her little baby had become so famous and important.

Ada had found out she was pregnant a few weeks before Jared's letter arrived. At first she'd been excited about the baby. She knew there would be people who disapproved, but as long as she had Jared, she could face anything.

Then Jared was gone, she was on her own, and she had no idea what she was going to do.

She had decided early on that she would keep her baby.

That wasn't the problem. The problem was, she didn't know how she would get by after the baby was born. She didn't have any family to rely on. Who would keep the baby when she had to go to work?

All these questions had weighed on her, making her sadness at losing Jared all the worse. Although she was strongly tempted, she decided that she would not get an abortion. It wasn't that she had religious reasons or that she thought it was a sin. She wasn't particularly religious at that time in her life.

Ada wanted to keep her baby because he would be all she would have to remember Jared.

They would face life together, Ada thought. *That was how it should be.*

And for a brief time, that was how it was.

As Ada lay there, waiting for sleep to take her, she began to hum and then to softly sing, "There is welcome for the sinner, and more graces for the good; there is mercy with the Savior; there is healing in his blood."

Chapter Ten

Ben was carrying an old shoebox when he came back into the room. He sat down in his recliner and sifted through the contents, finally pulling out several yellowed envelopes. He set the shoebox on the floor beside his chair and placed the envelopes in his lap.

"Martha only worked a few years out at the children's home. Times were tough, and we needed some extra income. One day as she was leaving, a young lady came up to her and asked whether or not the home was hiring. She said she was a good worker and needed the money.

"As a matter of fact, the home did need extra help, so Martha took her around to the front office and introduced her to the folks who ran the place. They hired her on, and she became sort of a general helper. She did kitchen work, cleaning, pretty much whatever needed to be done around the buildings."

I couldn't believe what I was hearing. "My mother worked at the home when I was there? How is that possible? I never saw her."

"That's what finally tipped off the administrators that

something strange was going on. Seems that she never wanted to be around when you were out and about. She always had some excuse for not wanting to serve the tables when you and the other children were eating. She preferred working the night shift, and if she did have to work days, she always wanted to be where the kids weren't."

"Working at a children's home, but not wanting to be around children," I said. "Okay, maybe a little out of the ordinary, but I wouldn't call it strange."

"That wasn't the strange part," Ben answered. "Even though she didn't want to be around the children, she was caught several times watching you from a distance. Sometimes you would be outside playing with other boys, and they'd find her standing in an upstairs window, just watching. She usually had an explanation, but eventually the administrators got curious. That's when they did a little investigating and found out she was your mother."

"Wait a minute," said Erica. "Wouldn't they already have known that? After all, she's the one who brought Jonathan to the home in the first place."

Ben shook his head. "That's not how children came to the home. They were wards of the state and sent to Kellner Home by the court."

"So they wouldn't have known who she was unless she told them," I said. "But why go and work there at the home?"

"She wanted to keep an eye on you," Ben replied. "See how you were doing. At least that's what she told them when they confronted her."

"What happened to her after that?" Erica asked.

"They fired her, of course, but decided not to prosecute." Ben looked down. "That's where my wife comes into the picture."

"What do you mean?" I asked.

"A few months after your mother was fired, she contacted Martha and asked for information about you. Simple stuff, like how you were doing in school. Were you growing? What did you like to eat? At first, Martha wouldn't tell her anything. She could have gotten fired if the administrators found out. But your mother wouldn't let it go, and Martha eventually had a choice to make."

"A choice?" I asked.

"She had to report your mother or give her the information she was asking for."

"I assume that she chose the latter."

Ben nodded. "She did."

"But why?"

"Martha put herself in your mother's place. She figured if she'd had to give up her own son, she'd probably want to check up on him from time to time, especially if he lived so close by. Bottom line, Martha didn't feel that she was doing any harm."

"How long did this go on?" I asked.

"A couple of years, as I recall. Then Martha found a job with better pay and easier hours."

I pointed to the envelopes on his lap. "What are those?"

Ben looked down at the letters. He placed his hand on them and sighed.

"After Martha quit working at the home, she obviously couldn't pass on any more information about you. Your mother must have gotten desperate. She took to hanging around the home and watching for you. Always at a distance, so you wouldn't see her. Finally, the home asked a judge to issue a restraining order. One night, not too long after that, they caught her inside the main building. She'd broken in and was standing in the hallway, looking into your room."

Ben turned his gaze toward me. His dark brown eyes had a world-weary look. "They arrested her, and the state eventually committed her to a mental health facility. She wrote a few letters to my wife from there. Martha answered them, but after a while your mother stopped writing. That was the last either of us ever heard from her."

Ben placed the letters on the coffee table in front of me.

"You can have them if you want," he said. "I don't know why Martha hung on to them all these years. I found them when I was clearing out her things and decided to keep them. I don't know why I did that. Maybe the Lord wanted me to save them for you."

I looked at the little pile of letters, and the longer I looked, the more confused and angry I felt.

"If she cared so much about me, why did she throw me away like a piece of trash?" I asked, not hiding the anger in my voice.

Erica put her hand on my forearm, and I shook it off.

"It wasn't like that," Ben replied.

"Then tell me what it was like," I said.

"She just wanted to be in your life," he said.

I shook my head as I stood up. "Uh-uh. I'm not buying it. If she loved me, she wouldn't have walked out on me."

I threw on my parka and stormed out the door and into

the cold night air. A few seconds later I heard Erica's muted voice from behind me. "Thank you for taking the time to help us, Pastor Morgan."

I was facing away from her and looking up into the night sky. Her boots made crunching sounds in the snow as she came up behind me.

"Well, that could have gone better," she said.

I didn't answer.

Above us, the aurora stretched across the sky, twisting and oscillating like a sparkling green ribbon. We stood there in the silence, watching it. As we gazed up at the display, I couldn't help wondering what compelled my mother to take such a great risk to be near me.

Could it possibly have been love?

Or was she merely trying to assuage a guilty conscience?

We drove in silence most of the way back to my hotel, and for that I was glad. I didn't need anyone to tell me that I'd blown it—again. That was the story of my life. For the most part I'm able to keep myself under control, but every now and then something will set me off. And when that happens, I'm not a very nice person to be around.

I was sorry Erica had seen that side of me and even sorrier that Ben had been on the receiving end of my rage. I'd go back and apologize to him.

I always did.

The worst part about my tantrum was that I'd stormed out

of the pastor's house without my mother's letters. They may have been helpful, but I would never know for certain now.

Erica turned a corner, and the hotel came into view about three blocks away. I knew I needed to say something before we parted.

I harbored no delusions that our relationship would ever be anything more than a friendship, but for a man like me, true friends are hard to come by. The irony of being wealthy and powerful is that you are surrounded by people most, if not all, of the time. But those people usually work for you, or they want something from you. It's rare when you find someone who is willing to accept you for who you are, someone who just enjoys being with you.

I didn't know if Erica could be that kind of person in my life, but it felt nice to have someone by my side who was not trying to get something out of me. Still, she was a reporter, and I did not intend to let down my guard completely. Not yet anyway.

We stopped at a red light about a block away from the hotel.

"I'm sorry about what happened back there," I said.

Erica looked straight ahead and, when the light turned, kept driving.

"I shouldn't have gone off on him like that. He was only trying to help."

Silence.

Erica pulled into the hotel parking lot and drove up to the front door.

"Look, I'm sorry. What else do you want me to say?"

Erica turned to me. "You think that's what it's all about, don't you? You blow up on someone who's trying to help you even though it's obvious that telling you those things is painful for him. And then you expect to throw out a cavalier 'I'm sorry,' 'mea culpa,' 'my bad,' and that will set everything right? You should have seen that man's face after you left. He wasn't just hurt; he was crushed. And why? Because he told you the truth."

"Look, Erica . . ."

"No, you look. I agreed to help you because I believe that you're doing the right thing. But I didn't agree to be a part of abusing people who tell you something you don't want to hear. Your temper is legendary, Mr. Jonathan 'Gold' Rush. It has inspired stories in every news outlet from CNN to the *National Enquirer*. But I have no intention of being a part of bulldozing people just because you get upset at something. You had better start controlling it if you want me to help you."

"I will. I promise."

Erica looked skeptical. "You've probably been promising to change for years and broken most of those promises. Just be forewarned. If you treat someone—anyone—like that again, I'm done. Got it?"

"Got it," I said.

I opened the door and got out of her car. There wasn't anything I could say in reply. She was absolutely right. "Will I see you tomorrow?" I asked.

"I'll be here at ten for breakfast. I've got some things I want to do before I come."

I was about to close the door when Erica shouted, "Wait a minute! I almost forgot." She unbuckled her seatbelt, reached into her coat, and pulled out five yellowed envelopes. "Here." She handed them to me. "Read through these before tomorrow morning. Maybe there will be something in them that can help us."

I held the envelopes up so the light from the carport fell across them. In the upper left corner of each, a name was scrawled. It was the name of the woman I was trying to learn about. The woman who gave birth to me.

Ada Guthrie.

***

Once I was back in my suite, I checked my BlackBerry for messages from Tim. Thankfully, there were none. It had been an exhausting day, and I wasn't up for any more confrontations or discussions about my behavior.

I sat down in a leather recliner and looked at the five envelopes. The return address was the Alaska Psychiatric Institute in Anchorage. They were postmarked in 1981 and 1982.

I was six years old when Ada Guthrie wrote them.

I could feel my heart beating harder as I held the envelopes. It felt strange to hold in my hands something that my mother had written.

I had no real mental picture of her, as she was little more than a shadow in my memories. My only clear recollection of her was her walking away after she abandoned me. That single memory had left me with a lifelong feeling that her leaving was my fault.

That memory still haunted my dreams.

Now I knew her name, but there was still no face.

I held on to the envelopes, almost afraid to read the letters. Afraid that in reading them I might discover that it really was my fault. That everything I had feared for so many years was true. That somehow I had forced my mother to give me up.

I sorted the envelopes by their postmark dates and took out the first letter. It was a single page, written on ruled school paper, similar to what a child in elementary school might use. It wasn't written in crayon, but it might as well have been. The handwriting, if you could call it that, looked like that of a fourth grader.

The letter was not dated:

Dear Martha,

I hope you are doing okay. They sent me here because I broke in to the children's home. I tried to tell them that I didn't mean any harm. I just wanted to see my boy and make sure he was okay. They didn't understand.

I guess it could be worse. They could have sent me to jail.

I worry about him all the time. He's so little. I'm afraid one of the bigger kids will hurt him. Jonathan shouldn't be there.

Thank you for everything you tried to do for me. You're the only true friend I have.

Your friend,
Ada

The words echoed in my mind: *Jonathan shouldn't be there.*

"But I'd have never ended up there if you hadn't left me. Why did you do it?"

I laid the letter on the side table and opened the next one. This one was dated May 13, 1981:

Dear Martha,

I've been here four months now, and I don't like this place very much. I feel like I'm in prison. I know they're reading my letters, so I have to be very careful about what I say or ask for.

I'd like to ask you for news about Jonathan, but I'll get in trouble if I do that. I imagine you don't have any news anyway since you don't work out there anymore.

I'm wondering if you might ever get down here to Anchorage. I'm allowed to have visitors, but I don't have any relatives or friends other than you. There are lots of people here, but I still get lonely.

Love,

Ada

I wondered whether Martha ever went down to Anchorage to visit Ada. Ben had not told us one way or the other. He did say that his wife wrote back to Ada. But Anchorage was at least 350 miles southwest of Fairbanks.

Something inside me hoped they had made the trip.

When I opened the third letter, I noticed a distinct

difference from the previous two. The tone was more upbeat. Even the handwriting was less childlike:

July 20, 1981

Dear Martha,

They're saying I'm doing a lot better and they'll be releasing me soon. I can't wait to get back home.

Is everybody doing okay? Any news about mutual friends?

Thank you for the letters and the birthday card you sent. They mean a lot to me. In all this time you're the only person who has written. Of course, I don't know who else would write. I don't have anybody out there who could send me a letter, except for a certain person that I'm not allowed to contact. It's okay, I guess. He probably doesn't even know I exist.

I'll write you as soon as I find out when I'm being released.

Oh, could you and your husband maybe come down and pick me up? I know it's a long drive and all, but I don't have any way to get back to Fairbanks.

I guess maybe they'll give me a bus ticket.

Thank you.

Your true friend,
Ada Guthrie

Did the people screening her mail notice the less-than-subtle reference to "mutual friends"? She was dying to ask for information about me, but that was clearly going to be a condition of her release. And if they did release her, did Ben and Martha make the long drive to Anchorage to bring Ada back to Fairbanks? I never met Martha, but based on the little bit of time I spent with Ben, I'd say that they probably did.

I glanced at the digital clock on the nightstand. The red LED numerals showed 10:28.

As I pulled the next letter from its envelope and unfolded it, I was immediately struck by how different it was from the others. The letter was undated, and her handwriting had degenerated to a practically illegible scrawl:

Dear Martha,

I'm not coming home. I don't understand. They've put me in prison and it's awful. Why won't they let me come home? I'll promise not to try to see Jonathan ever again. Can you find somebody to help me? Please?

I miss you,
Ada

I looked more carefully at the envelope. I hadn't noticed before, but the return address on this one was different from the previous letters. It was from the Hiland Mountain Correctional Center in Eagle River, Alaska. How did she go from a psychiatric hospital to a prison?

I took out the last of the five letters and unfolded it. It

was dated January 5, 1982. The handwriting was better, and the tone of the letter, although not upbeat, was not as panicked and confused as the previous one:

Dear Martha,

Thank you for the beautiful Christmas card. I've saved it as I've saved all the other cards you have sent. I can't tell you how much it means to me that you have not forgotten me.

It's been difficult adjusting to life here at Hiland Mountain, but I'm doing a lot better than I was when I first got here. I couldn't understand why they weren't letting me go home after I finished my treatments, but I do now. I'll be up for parole at the end of this year, and if I don't get in trouble before then, there's a good chance I might make it.

I'm so sorry for all the trouble I've caused everyone. Especially Jonathan.

I wish I could turn the clock back and make things better, but I know that can't happen. I just hope that my bad decisions don't mess up Jonathan's life too much.

Oh, by the way, you'll be glad to know that I'm going to church now. My cellie is a Christian, and she invited me to go with her. I like the singing a lot (although I'm not a very good singer). One of my favorites is a song called "There's a Wideness in God's Mercy." I'm trying to memorize that one, but it's going kind of slow.

The chaplain gave me a Bible to read. I'm trying,

71

but I don't understand much of it. Maybe when I get out, you can help me.

I hope you can visit me again when the weather warms up. I know it's a long drive from Fairbanks, but I so enjoy sitting and talking with you, even if it is for just a short time.

Well, I'd better finish this so I can get it in the mail.

Love,

Ada

I sat there for a long time, holding Ada's letter in my hands. Reading it again and again. For the first time in years, I didn't know how I felt about her. I'd spent half a lifetime hating this woman for walking out on me. As far as I was concerned, she couldn't have loved me because if she had, she'd never have left me. Now I had in my possession letters that told a different story.

The problem was, the story was incomplete. I still didn't know why she'd given me up. But I did know one thing. Whatever her faults or crimes, Ada Guthrie had loved me.

And that meant it wasn't my fault.

Chapter Eleven

The clock on the far wall showed nine forty-five. Ada had been at the Chena Resort's restaurant for almost three hours. She had a clear view of the main entrance, so if Jonathan came down for breakfast, she would see him.

Ada knew that she would have no problem recognizing her famous son. Even though she had seen his picture on TV and in the newspapers and magazines, she wondered what it would be like to see him in person.

From her vantage point in the back corner, she could see every table. Of course, Ada knew that Jonathan might decide to eat somewhere else or even have breakfast in his room. But she couldn't watch every restaurant in Fairbanks. If this didn't work, she would have to think of something different.

Ada sipped her coffee, keeping her eyes fixed on the front entrance.

"Would you like me to warm that up for you?" a voice broke in. Her waiter—they called them servers now—stood by her table with a fresh pot of coffee.

Ada nodded and smiled, then quickly looked away.

"Very good," he said as he refilled what would now be her sixth cup of coffee.

As the young man walked away, Ada watched him. He was a handsome young man, and she was surprised at how nice he had been to her. She had never been in this restaurant before, but she had looked through its big windows. After that, she never tried coming in. One look at the expensive furnishings and the well-dressed people inside, and Ada figured she would never get past the front door.

Fairbanks didn't have a lot of ritzy restaurants like the big cities do, but there were places where someone like Ada would feel uncomfortable. If it hadn't been for Jonathan, she wouldn't be here now. She had been half afraid they would slam the door in her face, but it was worth risking rejection just to get a glimpse of her son.

Ada heard some muffled voices, and then someone said, "Right this way."

She looked back toward the entrance, and her mouth went dry. Her heart started beating so hard she could feel it in her ears.

There was her Jonathan, following the hostess to a table.

Ada wanted to get a drink of water to wet her mouth, but her hands were shaking so badly she was afraid she'd spill it everywhere and draw attention to herself. Tears started to fill her eyes, and she tried to blink them away because they were blurring her vision. She took one of the linen napkins and dabbed her eyes.

He sat down at a table clear across the restaurant and took a chair that was sideways to hers. That was good because she

could look at him as much as she wanted without him notic-
ing her. He was everything she'd expected him to be, and so
much more handsome in person than on TV.

She wondered what it would be like to hug him, to hold
him. It had been thirty-one years since she had touched his
tear-stained face and told him she had to leave.

She would never forget that day as long as she lived.

And now, here she was, sitting halfway across a room
from him, and she couldn't approach him. Part of her wanted
to run over to his table and tell him who she was and how
much she loved him. But Ada knew that could never be.

She could never face him, and even if she did, how would
she explain what she had done that horrible day? What
excuse could a mother give for abandoning her child?

"Are you all right, ma'am?"

The young man's voice startled Ada, and she flinched,
nearly knocking over her water glass. Her server stood there,
a concerned look on his face.

"What?" she asked.

"You're crying," he said. "Are you all right? Is there anything I can do for you?"

"No," she said, shaking her head. "I'm okay. I'm okay."
She managed a weak smile.

The young man nodded and went back to his work.

Ada felt the emotions rising in her, and she knew she had
to leave. Thirty-one years of grief and shame were bubbling
to the top and would soon spill over. She couldn't be near
Jonathan when it happened.

She took out what was left of her money, keeping enough

for bus fare back to her home, and laid it on the table. Tears flowed freely as she stood up and made her way to the exit.

She heard her server's voice calling "thank you" behind her.

When she reached the exit, Ada turned around and took one last look at Jonathan's table. He was reading a copy of *USA Today*. She stood there for a moment, letting her eyes soak in this image of her son.

As far as she knew, this would be the last time she would ever be this close to him.

Chapter Twelve

It was 10:30 a.m., and I was finished with breakfast and half-way through the business section of *USA Today* when Erica finally showed up.

"You're late," I said with a grin. "If you were my employee, I'd fire you."

"If I were your employee, I'd have already quit," she retorted.

"Touché."

She pulled out a chair and sat down. "My errands took a little longer than I'd expected. But I think you'll be happy with what I've found."

"I could use a little good news," I said. "My company's stock is down ten points." I folded my paper and said, "So what did you find out?"

"I had some friends at the police station and courthouse dig up whatever they could find about Ada Guthrie."

"And?"

"After she broke in to the Kellner Home, she was arrested and charged with breaking and entering. Usually, that kind of charge wouldn't have drawn a very severe penalty, especially with it being her first offense. But they didn't have antistalking laws back then, and somebody evidently felt she was a threat to the children's safety. So they threw the book at her. If she hadn't had a history of hanging around the children's home, and if they hadn't found her standing at the door of your bedroom, she probably would have gotten a much lighter sentence."

"But they committed her to a psychiatric facility. How did she end up in prison?" I asked.

Erica waved down the server. "Coffee, please. And could I have a cherry Danish with that? Thanks."

She turned back to me. "Her attorney pursued an insanity defense, but Alaska is one of the few states with a 'guilty but mentally ill' statute. Rather than find someone not guilty by reason of insanity, a jury can find the person guilty but mentally ill."

"What does that mean?" I asked.

"If you're found to be guilty but mentally ill, you go to a psychiatric facility first. After they decide you're 'cured,' then you go to a prison for the remainder of your sentence."

The server brought Erica's coffee and pastry. "Thank you," she said. "I'm starved."

"That explains what Ada wrote in her letters," I said. "She was expecting to be released when her treatment was over and couldn't understand why they sent her to prison. So how long was she in?"

"She was paroled to Fairbanks in 1984. After her parole was up, she dropped off the map. She hasn't been in any more trouble, but no one seems to know where she is. I managed to get her last known address, for what that's worth."

"Do you think she's still alive?" I asked.

Erica shrugged as she took the last bite of her Danish and chased it with coffee. A little icing stuck to her cheek. I pointed to the same spot on my cheek and handed her a napkin.

She flushed and grinned sheepishly as she wiped off the icing. "Sorry. I didn't mean to gobble it down so fast. I checked the death records and couldn't find anything, but for all we know, she might have moved somewhere else."

"So we've come to a dead end," I said. "She may be alive, but nobody's seen her in years. Did you find out anything else?"

"I had my friend check the family court records. There wasn't much she could find other than that Ada Guthrie voluntarily signed away her parental rights when you were four, but you probably already knew that."

I nodded. "I just wish I knew why," I said. "That's the crazy part about this whole deal. She voluntarily gives me up, but then is so obsessed with me that she takes every opportunity to hang around the children's home. Finally, she totally loses it and breaks into the home so she can watch me sleep."

"It sounds like a total mental breakdown," Erica said.

"I agree. But why? Seems to me that if she didn't want me anymore, she'd have been happy to get rid of me."

"Maybe it wasn't as simple as that. Maybe she didn't have a choice."

"I guess we'll never know," I said.

Erica shook her head. "I'm not letting you give up that easily. At least not until we've checked out this address."

"Let's go then," I said.

"My car awaits," Erica replied.

"Not this time. My driver's outside, and he's got my SUV all warmed up."

"What? You don't like riding in my little Corolla?"

"Let's just say I find it confining," I said.

It was almost noon, but the midday sun tracked low in the sky, casting long shadows and giving the landscape a late-afternoon appearance. The drive out to Farmers Loop Road wouldn't be a long one. Only about fifteen minutes. According to Erica, Ada Guthrie's last known address was a dry cabin somewhere off Ski Boot Hill Road, in the north part of the city.

Erica and I sat in the back of the Jeep as Ryan drove.

"So how'd you end up in Miami?" Erica asked. "That's quite a change for someone born in Alaska."

I laughed. "For that, I can blame my adoptive parents. I was nine when Gary and Sandra Rush adopted me."

"Were they from Miami?" Erica asked.

"Yes."

"Did they come all the way up here just to adopt you?"

"Not likely," I said. "I wasn't the most lovable child at the home. By the time I was nine, I'd grown into quite a little hellion. If they'd had a 'least likely to be adopted list,' I'd have probably been in the number one spot."

"So what, they were just people who liked a challenge?"

"Well, they were certainly that. But they were also two

of the kindest and most gracious people I ever knew. They loved me unconditionally, and every time I did something to try to drive them away, they just forgave me and kept on loving me."

"I bet they're proud of you and what you've accomplished," Erica said.

"They would have been," I replied. "They died in an auto accident about ten years ago."

"I'm sorry," she said.

"It's up here on the right," Ryan called over his shoulder.

I looked out the window. In the few minutes we had been talking, the landscape had changed from urban to rural. Instead of houses and buildings, now tall snow-covered pine trees lined both sides of the road.

Ryan slowed down and turned off the main road. As we rolled along, I could see smaller side roads leading into the trees. Occasionally, I saw a driveway branching off toward a cabin.

"We're on Ski Boot Hill Road now," Ryan said.

We turned onto an even smaller road, and soon we came upon a short driveway leading to the left and down a hill. Deep snow covered the driveway. The trees were so thick, we couldn't see the cabin from the road, but it was obvious that nobody had come up or down the driveway in quite a while.

"This can't be it," said Erica.

"Can you get us down there?" I asked.

"I think so," Ryan said. He engaged the four-wheel drive and turned down the driveway.

The Jeep chewed through the snow as Ryan guided it down the driveway and deeper into the property. We came around a short curve and found the cabin. Or what was left of it.

A blanket of snow covered the skeleton of what had once been Ada Guthrie's cabin. Blackened wall studs, capped with snow, jutted from what had once been the structure's floor. On the far corner, part of one wall still stood. At the front, I could see the peak of the roof, although the wall beneath it had collapsed.

The shed and the outhouse looked intact, but also deserted.

"I don't think we need to get out," I said. "Take us back to the road."

Ryan managed to turn the Jeep around and drive back up to the road. "Where would you like to go now, sir?" he asked.

"The hotel, I guess. I've had enough fun with all this. I'm ready to go home."

"We're not giving up yet," Erica said.

It was not a question.

"What?"

"We're not giving up yet," she repeated, this time more forcefully. "Fairbanks isn't like Miami, where good fences make good neighbors. People know each other up here. They actually talk to each other, make friends, and help each other."

"Meaning what?" I asked.

"If Ada Guthrie lived in that cabin, chances are pretty good her neighbors knew her. And they might even know where she's gone. Ryan, I saw another driveway just a little bit farther on the left. Let's drive up there and see if anybody's home."

Ryan looked at me.

"You heard the lady," I said. "Let's see if anybody's home."

He grinned. "Yes, sir."

<hr />

The next cabin up the road wasn't much bigger than Ada's, and there was definitely somebody home. A column of smoke trailed up from a chimney and into the blue sky. There were no vehicles around the place and no tire tracks on the driveway. But there was a footpath through the snow, leading up to the main road. There were also large paw prints all around the building.

"They've got a big dog," I said, pointing at the prints.

"Most everybody does up here," Erica said.

The building was narrow and long and old. This was not a cabin built by someone with a lot of money, who wanted luxurious living. From the outside, at least, it appeared sparse and utilitarian, the kind of place you might expect a grizzled old trapper to live.

When we knocked at the door, we were greeted by a thunderous deep bark.

"Correction," I said. "A very big dog."

The dog continued barking, but nobody answered the door.

Erica knocked again. "Hello? Is anybody home? We need some help."

We heard a muffled voice: "Just a minute. Just a minute."

The dog kept barking, but it sounded farther away now.

I assumed the owner was putting it somewhere so it couldn't attack us. At least that's what I hoped.

A few seconds later, the door opened a crack. I could see only part of a weathered face, a dark brown eye framed by matted black hair. "Yes?" The voice was thick and gravelly, like someone who has smoked a lifetime of cigarettes. It was also without question a woman's voice.

"Hi. I'm Erica, and this is Jonathan. Could we ask you a few questions?"

"What about?" the woman asked.

"We're trying to find a Mrs. Ada Guthrie. She was supposed to be living in the cabin next door, but it's burned out. We'd really like to find her if we can. Do you know Ada?"

The door opened a little more, just barely enough for me to see her round face. She looked at me, then Erica, then back at me. Then she nodded. "I know Ada."

Erica threw me an I-told-you-so grin. "Do you know where she lives?"

The little woman hesitated a few seconds, then said, "Ada's gone."

"You mean she's dead?" Erica asked.

"Not dead. Just gone," the woman answered.

"Can you tell us where she is? We need to find her."

The woman shook her head. "Can't help you," she said as she started to push the door closed.

I put my hand on the door to keep her from shutting it all the way. A look of fear flooded the little woman's eyes.

"I'm not going to hurt you," I said. "Please don't close the door yet. We didn't mean to frighten you. It's very important that we find Ada Guthrie. She's my mother, and I really need to talk to her. Do you have any idea where she is?"

"Maybe."

"Could you help me find her?"

She shook her head.

"Why not?" Erica asked.

"Ada don't want to be found," she answered.

"Can you tell me your name, at least?" asked Erica.

The woman looked at Erica as if sizing her up, trying to decide if she could be trusted with this information.

"Mercy," she said. "My name is Mercy."

"Mercy," Erica repeated. "That's a beautiful name. Could we come inside to visit? It's awfully cold out here."

Mercy shook her head. "No. No one comes in."

Erica smiled and said, "That's okay. Thank you for talking to us, Mercy. We're going to leave now."

Mercy nodded, glanced my way one more time, and then closed the door. Seconds later, I heard the big dog barking again.

"Let's go," Erica said.

"What do you mean, 'Let's go'?" I said. "She knows where Ada lives. She as much said so."

"No. It's time to go," Erica said. "I'll explain later." She turned away from the cabin and walked back to the Jeep.

As Ryan drove us away from the little cabin and back toward Fairbanks, I said, "I don't understand. You're the one who wanted to check out the neighbors. Now we found someone and you're just going back to town?"

Erica smiled and said, "You may be a hotshot CEO, but you don't know anything about cultivating a source."

I gave her a puzzled look. "What?"

"I'm a reporter. Persuading people to talk to me is what I do for a living. That lady is frightened and suspicious, particularly of you. If we come on too strong, she's going to shut down on us completely. I know you're in a hurry, but we have to take our time."

I sighed. "All right. You're the expert. So what do we do next?"

"Ryan," said Erica, "take us to the grocery store."

Chapter Thirteen

Ada Guthrie's dream had come true. She had been able to see her son again. In person this time, not on TV or in a magazine. It was something she never expected to happen.

She sat down in her rocker and put her scrapbook in her lap. She didn't have very many pictures of Jonathan from when he was little. She'd taken plenty during those first few years, but since she had no family, most of her things had gotten lost or stolen while she was away. After she got out and came back to Fairbanks, she'd managed to find a few photos.

She opened the tattered scrapbook to the first page.

The tape that held the four baby pictures was now stiff and yellow. A few pieces had fallen off, leaving marks on the corners of the photos.

Someone had taken these pictures at the hospital. Jonathan looked so cute, all bundled up for the cold weather. Jonathan had been such a beautiful baby. Chubby cheeks and coal black hair. Even back then, he looked like his daddy.

Of course, everybody told Ada how much Jonathan looked like her, but she knew different. They only said that because they didn't want to say anything that would remind her of Jared and make her cry.

But Ada knew.

Little Jonathan was his daddy through and through.

It wasn't too big of a problem early on, but the older he got, the more he looked like Jared. By the time he was four, he looked like his daddy in miniature.

He even talked like him.

Ada had been trying to put Jared behind her and get on with her life, and for the most part she'd done a pretty good job of it. She'd been able to keep her waitress job at Big Merv's; she just brought Jonathan along with her. Big Merv's wife, Audrey, liked to play the grandma, since she didn't have any grandchildren of her own.

That worked pretty well until Jonathan got older.

She flipped over to the next page. The pictures there were of Jonathan when he was a toddler. Playing with blocks. Swimming in the little wading pool she'd bought. Riding on his tricycle. The last was when he was four years old. They were at Alaskaland, standing in front of an old cabin in Gold Rush Town.

Such a beautiful boy. So much like his daddy.

Too much like his daddy.

She'd tried so hard to forget about Jared, but his leaving had scarred her deeply. And now, with every passing day Jonathan looked a little more like him. And as much as she loved her son, his presence in her daily life had become pure torture.

Finally, she'd decided she had to do something.

It was the most painful decision she'd ever made in her life.

She'd bundled him up and gone downtown to the courthouse. Somebody there directed her to the child welfare office. She'd told them that she couldn't take care of Jonathan anymore and wanted to put him up for adoption.

They tried to talk her out of it, even made her go to counseling. But she stood her ground.

"I can't do it anymore," she told them. "Every time I look at him, I see the man who tore my heart out. It hurts too much to have him around."

Eventually, the people at child welfare were convinced she was telling the truth, and they let her sign away her parental rights. There were lots of papers to sign and lawyers to talk to. She even had to go before a judge. But when it was all said and done, she left him there at the courthouse.

She told him that the people there would take good care of him and that he shouldn't cry.

Then she turned around and left. Just like that.

It was the worst mistake of her life.

Chapter Fourteen

"If you want this lady to open up to you, you'll have to earn her trust," Erica said. "You can't just go barging into her home and demand information like you're interrogating her for a crime."

I wheeled a half-full shopping cart through Walmart's grocery section. Erica had piled in a generous helping of coffee, dry and canned goods, and other items that had long shelf lives. Now we were cruising through the meat and produce section.

"So you think that giving her all this stuff is going to make her open up and tell us what she knows about Ada?"

Erica shrugged. "It may and it may not. It could take a while before she trusts us enough to open up."

"Could you define 'a while'?" I asked.

"On a few occasions, I've taken months to develop sources."

"Months? You've got to be kidding. I can't stay up here for months. I have a business to run."

Erica rolled her eyes. "I find it difficult to believe that the third largest software company in America is going to collapse just because you're away for a few months."

"You may be a hotshot reporter," I said, "but you don't know anything about how a business operates on this level. True, the company can run without me there, but investors get nervous if the one who developed the whole thing disappears. I can't be gone indefinitely. They are just now getting over my overdose six months ago."

Erica pulled a large roast out of the cooler and dropped it into the cart. "Relax," she said. "I was just pushing your buttons. Although it's true that I've taken months to develop some sources, it usually doesn't take that long. And I think in this case, it will go a lot faster."

"How fast?"

"I think we can find out what we need to know pretty quickly. Two or three visits probably. The key is in making her feel comfortable and safe. You've got to let her feel like she's in control."

Erica put a five-pound wheel of cheddar cheese on top of the other food items. "That should do it for here," she said. "Now, let's head over to the pet section."

"Pets? What for?"

She grinned. "To get a fifty-pound sack of the best dog food they've got."

⬧

We checked out and loaded our purchases into the Cherokee, and Ryan had us out on the road again.

"Take us back to Mercy's house," Erica said.

As we settled back into our seats, I said, "I can't remember the last time I shopped for groceries. I'm not sure I'd have known how if you hadn't been there."

"Were the people who adopted you rich?"

"Very," I said. "But they weren't snobby rich, if you know what I mean. They had money, but they used it to do good. They had a lot of love to spread around. I was one of ten children they adopted over the years. All of us were special needs, one way or another."

"Ten adopted children? Did they have any of their own?"

"No. They weren't able. There was so much love there, they went out and found children who needed them. I have three brothers and six sisters."

"You were special needs?"

"My brothers and sisters all have physical disabilities. My needs were emotional. I couldn't handle my anger at being abandoned, so I acted out. A lot."

"So how did they manage to find you all the way up here?" Erica asked.

"They were on vacation. Brought the whole family to experience the Trans-Alaska Railroad. When they were in Fairbanks, they heard about the Kellner Home and decided to stop by."

"And it was love at first sight?"

"More like love at first fright," I said. "As I recall, I put on a particularly vivid display of temper that day. The way my mother told the story, I was not happy with the menu the evening they visited and I threw a full-blown tantrum, which included throwing my dinner plate and food across the dining room."

I smiled at Erica. "She said they knew right then that they were going to adopt me. Crazy, huh?"

"Sounds pretty nice to me. So how did living with them work out? They obviously didn't pack you up and ship you back to Alaska."

"Well, there were rough spots," I said. "But as time passed, there were fewer and fewer of them. It was awfully difficult to resist their love. They just kept forgiving me."

"So if they helped you get past your anger, why are you up here now?"

"I started struggling with it again not too long after my parents died. Little things would set me off. At first, I ignored it because most of the time I thought my anger was justified. People at the company would screw up, and I'd unload on them. Stuff like that. But as time passed it took less and less to trigger an outburst. I wasn't much fun to live with."

"That's what broke up your marriages?" Erica asked.

"Pretty much," I said. "Over the last decade I've become what they call a 'toxic' person."

"So what finally turned the tables? What convinced you that you needed help?"

"After my second marriage broke up, I took up motorcycle riding. Based on the way I rode it, I think I had a death wish, even back then. It would be generous to say I was reckless. I crashed one afternoon on a slick road. Broke my right leg in three places."

"I remember hearing about that," Erica said.

"They did surgery, put in a steel rod. That began my love affair with painkillers. Everything went downhill after that.

I managed to get married a third time. That's not difficult when you've got as much money as I do."

Erica nodded. There was something about the way she was looking at me that made me pause. It wasn't sympathy. And she wasn't listening like a reporter. Something in her eyes told me she cared about what I was telling her.

"My third marriage lasted all of six months. Janice couldn't deal with my tendency to throw expensive things across the room when I was having a tantrum. By that time, pills were running my life."

"Alcohol too?" Erica asked.

I shook my head. "No. I've never been much of a drinker. A little wine now and then, but that's about it. But the pills more than made up for the absence of alcohol.

"After Janice left, the bottom fell out for me emotionally. I checked into a cheap motel one evening. Filled the bathtub, took an overdose of pills, and slashed my wrists. I'm sure you heard about that. It was all over the tabloids."

"I wrote the story for the *Miner*," she said. "Anything that happens to you is news up here. You're a hometown celebrity."

"Then you know how I was rescued."

"Only that the police were sent to the motel and they found you."

I looked out the window. Tall pine trees swept by us as we turned onto Mercy's road.

"I was supposed to be at a meeting that evening. When I didn't show, they tried to call my cell phone and didn't get an answer. I'm obsessive about staying in touch with the people who run my company, so when they couldn't reach me, they got worried. My cell phone was still turned on even though I wasn't answering it, and they were able to track it down to the motel and send someone out to check on me.

"After I was released from the hospital, the board of directors and a few good friends packed me off to the Betty Ford Clinic. They got me off the pills. I tried to go back to work, but I was having problems coping with life. One of my board members suggested I talk to his pastor, Tim Moser. I'd never been into religion much, but by then I was getting pretty desperate."

"So you've experienced a religious conversion?" She made little quotation marks with her fingers when she said the word *conversion*.

"Well, I guess you could say I'm still on the way. A lot of what Tim says about Jesus makes sense. And I've been going to his church every Sunday for a few months. Tim is the one who sent me up here."

"What does he think you'll accomplish?"

I shrugged. "All I know is that he's convinced that the seed of my anger was planted here in Fairbanks when I was four. And he says that if I don't deal with it, it will destroy me."

"Sounds reasonable," said Erica.

"I'm still not convinced," I replied.

"Why not?"

"I don't see how understanding my mother's reasons for her actions will make any difference. Look, if someone had tried to murder me, how would it help me to know why he did it?"

Erica looked skeptical. "She didn't try to murder you, Jonathan."

"That's not the point," I said. "Tim's no dummy, and neither am I. The only way I'll get rid of this anger is to forgive her. And I don't think that I'll ever be able to do that."

Erica was about to reply, but before she could, Ryan called over his shoulder, "We're here."

<hr />

Erica carried the bag of milk and cheese, and I hoisted the huge sack of dog food onto my shoulder. Together we made our way through the snow and back to Mercy's front door. Ryan stayed in the Jeep because Erica thought that Mercy might be frightened to have all three of us at her door.

"Should I go back and get the rest of the food?" I asked.

Erica shook her head. "We don't want to overwhelm her. It's probably going to take more than one visit to get her to talk to us. We'll bring a little each time we come."

I groaned quietly. Why couldn't we get this done quickly? Did we really have to drag it out?

Erica knocked at the door. Just like the last time, we heard the dog's loud barking at the door, and then it became fainter as Mercy closed off the dog in another room. After a few minutes she opened the door a crack and peered out at us. She didn't appear frightened this time or even particularly surprised to see us again so soon.

"Hi, Mercy," Erica said in a cheery voice. "We brought some food for you."

"And your dog," I added, pointing to the fifty-pound sack that rested uncomfortably on my shoulder.

Mercy looked at us for a few seconds, her eyes flicking from Erica to me, then back to Erica. Finally, she stepped back from the door and opened it wide enough for us to enter. We went inside, bringing a blast of subzero air with us. She quickly shut the door and rolled a heavy throw rug against it.

The layout of the cabin looked simple. The building was long and narrow, like a trailer house, but a lot more solid. The living room was just inside the front door. After that was a kitchen and dining area, then a short hallway back to the bedroom.

All the furniture appeared to be handmade. Even the sofa was constructed from what looked like hand-hewn logs and tree branches. The coffee table was the remnants of a very large tree stump.

Erica followed Mercy into the kitchen area and placed the bag of food on the table. Mercy helped her unload the items and put them into her old refrigerator. She didn't seem to be the least bit offended by our offer of food.

It was the first time I'd seen Mercy other than through a tiny crack. She was short and round, but she didn't look fat. Living in Alaska required toughness, and Mercy looked tough. The skin of her face and hands was dark and weathered, and her deep brown eyes spoke silently of a hard life.

"Where should we put the dog food?" Erica asked.

"Over here," Mercy said in her gravelly voice.

She walked over to a door and opened it. Behind the door was a pantry the size of a walk-in closet. I followed her and set the sack down by the other dog food. Judging by the brand of food that was already there, Mercy's dog was going to experience a huge jump in quality dining.

She smiled and patted the sack. "He'll like that," Mercy said. "Yes, indeed. He'll like that."

Then Mercy did something I never suspected. She motioned toward the living room and said, "Sit down. Sit down."

Erica smiled at me and gave me a little thumbs-up as we went over to the sofa.

The upholstery was threadbare, and in a few places the stuffing was poking out, but aside from that the homemade sofa was quite comfortable. Mercy bustled about in the kitchen and soon came out with a tray and three mugs of coffee. None of the mugs matched. One was from a Holiday Inn, one from a hospital, and the third from a car dealership.

I took the Holiday Inn mug.

Mercy sat down in a rocking chair—also homemade— across from us. The expression on her face was strange. It was like she felt she should be hospitable, perhaps, since we had brought her the food, but she wasn't totally comfortable with our presence either.

I thought Erica would spend some time breaking the ice. Instead, she spoke softly and gently, "Mercy, do you remember why we came?"

Mercy nodded. "You want to know about Ada."

"That's right. How long ago did her cabin burn down?"

Mercy closed her eyes and spoke quietly, as if talking to herself. "Long time. Long time."

"What happened?" asked Erica.

Mercy opened her eyes. "Ada's wood stove caught fire and burned the cabin down. It was sad."

"I imagine it was," Erica replied. "Was Ada hurt?"

Mercy closed her eyes again. "No," she said, shaking her head. "Ada was okay. She was okay."

"What did she do after the fire?" Erica asked. "Where did she live?"

"A friend. She lived with a friend."

"Do you know where Ada's friend lives? We'd very much like to talk to her."

A look of sadness crossed Mercy's face. "No. Ada's friend died."

"I'm sorry," said Erica. "So what did Ada do?"

"Ada was very sad."

"Did she move somewhere else?" I broke in. "Can you tell us where to find her?'

Mercy didn't answer. She just closed her eyes and sat there.

"Jonathan." Erica looked at me and shook her head.

I knew what she was saying, but the snail's pace of the conversation was driving me crazy.

"Mercy," Erica said, changing the subject, "have you lived in Fairbanks all your life?"

Mercy opened her eyes and nodded.

"Me too," said Erica. Then she flashed a sidelong glance at me. "Or at least most of it. But I was born here, and I grew up here. And I don't plan on leaving. How about you?"

Mercy shook her head. "I don't want to leave. Ever."

"So tell me about your family. Were your parents lifelong Alaskans too?"

"Mother was," said Mercy. "Never met my father."

"Oh?" said Erica.

Mercy nodded. A look of deep sadness, almost pain, crossed her already careworn face. "He came up for the gold rush." Her dark face flushed, and she looked down at the floor. "He left soon after I was born." She shook her head, still looking at the floor. "Never met him."

We sat silently together for a few minutes.

It was the first time I had felt sorry for someone other than myself in a long time. The world of big business had hardened me over the years. Mine was a cutthroat world where empathy often was a sign of weakness. But here was a woman with whom I could empathize. We had a shared experience: being abandoned by a parent. True, she hadn't been born when it happened, and she had no memories of the abandonment, but I could tell it disturbed her. She may not have had the memories, but the pain was still there.

I felt a kinship with Mercy.

I also realized that kinship could be the way to get her to tell me about my mother.

I drained my coffee cup. "Mercy, may I ask you a question?"

She nodded.

"Would you go out to eat with us tomorrow night? I'd like to take you and Erica someplace special."

Mercy's eyes widened. I couldn't quite tell whether it was out of fear or excitement. She didn't answer right away.

She looked down at the old pants she was wearing. "I don't have any nice clothes."

"You don't need them. As far as I'm concerned, you look like a queen."

Mercy's face flushed again. "Okay," she said in a tiny voice.

"We'd better go," Erica said, standing to leave.

"We'll see you about five tomorrow," I said. "Okay?"

Mercy nodded and gave me a hint of a smile.

Back in the Jeep, as Ryan drove us back to Fairbanks, Erica said, "Good job. We made great progress. And offering to take her out to eat is perfect, not to mention very thoughtful. You're getting the hang of this. I might make a reporter out of you yet."

As the Jeep rolled on toward Fairbanks, Erica reached over and put her hand in mine.

Chapter Fifteen

Ada Guthrie had seen her son up close for the first time since he was a little boy. It was a dream come true. But it also created a problem. Maybe she was being silly. After all, Fairbanks was a city of thirty-five thousand people. Just because Jonathan was moving back here didn't mean she had to leave. Not really.

But if Jonathan came back here to live, he would be in the news more. And people would be talking about him all the time.

She had been watching Jonathan from a distance—a safe distance—for years. But for him to be so close, that would be too much. It would be a daily reminder of the worst decision of her life and all the mistakes that followed it—mistakes that led to her being in a mental hospital, then prison.

The only good thing that had come from prison was that she came to know the Lord. She knew that God had forgiven her for abandoning her son.

But Ada could never forgive herself.

As much as she hated to think about such a thing, maybe it was time for her to find a new place to live.

Ada pulled an old suitcase from her bedroom closet. The suitcase wasn't very big. Nor was it in good condition. She needed to put a strap around it to keep it closed, but it was all she had. She wasn't sure why she had even bought it. She picked it up at a flea market about ten years ago. Since then she mainly used it to store flour, rice, and other dry goods that she wanted to protect from the mice.

But now it was time to empty it out. She opened the suitcase on her bed and took out the sacks of food that filled it.

She had no idea where she would go or how she would get there. But it would have to be far enough away so that she would not be reminded every day about her selfishness in signing away her parental rights and walking out on her son.

She regretted her decision to give up Jonathan the moment she went through the family courtroom door. How could she turn her back on that sweet little boy? What did he do to deserve that? Now poor little Jonathan had been abandoned not once but twice. His daddy had left him before he was ever born, and now she was leaving him too.

She remembered going home that day. The house seemed so empty. She walked into his bedroom and sat down on his little bed. His toys were still scattered about. She picked up Jonathan's tiny brown teddy bear and hugged it. Why hadn't she thought to bring that with him to the courthouse?

Ada curled up on Jonathan's bed that day and cried herself to sleep.

The next day she got some boxes and packed up all his

toys and clothes. She told herself that she would eventually take them to the courthouse, so they could take them to him. But she never did. She kept his belongings in the closet, and they stayed with her until her house burned down years later.

Her guilt was so great that the only way she could deal with it was to try to drown it out. She went out with her friends. She partied. She enjoyed her newfound freedom from responsibility.

As the months passed, she got to the point that sometimes she could go a whole day and not think about Jonathan. She did everything she could to drive him from her mind. And eventually, she was successful.

But then the dreams started.

She found herself waking up, crying in the middle of the night. She would dream that she and Jonathan were together, playing at Pioneer Park, running together through the gold rush village. Jonathan would turn around and tell her how much he loved her, but before she could give him a hug, someone would run up and snatch him away. She could never see the person's face, but she always heard Jonathan screaming in the distance.

That's when she knew she had to see him again. But how? They wouldn't tell her where he was living, so she started watching the preschools and day-care centers. There weren't that many of them in Fairbanks, so she figured that sooner or later she would see Jonathan.

It took a few weeks, but she finally spotted him coming

out of the Wee Ones Preschool and getting into a car. She followed it to the Kellner Children's Home.

She started walking by the home and watching the children playing outside. When she saw Jonathan safe, running and playing with the other children, his long black hair blowing in the wind, she relaxed, and the dreams went away for a while.

But they always came back.

Ada began to wonder whether there was a way she could get closer to him, see him more often. She knew that Martha Morgan worked up there as a cook. Maybe she could get a job at the home.

That's where her life began to fall apart.

She had been able to get a job at the home and, although it was difficult, managed to keep watch on Jonathan without him seeing her. She knew that she couldn't let him see her because he wouldn't understand why he couldn't go home with her. So she contented herself with watching him from a distance.

That worked well until the people who ran the home found out who she was.

They fired her, of course.

Not long after that, the dreams started again. But this time they were worse.

She and Jonathan were ice skating on the Chena River, and the ice started to break up, separating them. She watched helplessly as the river took her son away.

It wasn't long before she was waking up every night with the same dream.

She tried to walk by the home like she used to so she

could see Jonathan when he was playing outside. But this time they were watching for her. They called the police several times and finally got a restraining order to keep her away from their property.

She tried to obey, to stay away. But she couldn't stop the dreams.

She needed to see him just one more time. Make sure he was all right. So one night after awakening from the same nightmare, she went up to the home and broke in through the kitchen door. It was an old door on an older building, and jimmying the lock wasn't difficult. Everyone was asleep as she tiptoed up to the second floor.

She knew where Jonathan's room was, and she walked quietly down the hall and opened his door. Jonathan and his roommate were asleep in their beds. Ada just stood there, taking in the sight of her son.

But somebody must have heard her because soon voices came from downstairs. They had found the jimmied door. A police officer came running up the steps and down the hallway.

They arrested Ada and put her on trial. They said she was crazy and sent her away.

They didn't understand.

She just had to know he was all right.

Ada closed her suitcase. She was ready to leave, but she had one more thing to do. She knew she couldn't leave without writing Jonathan a letter and asking for his forgiveness. She knew it was something she would never be able to do face-to-face. Ada was painfully shy and became tongue-tied when she tried to talk to people. But she could write her thoughts down in a letter and mail it to him.

She took out a piece of notebook paper and sat down at her kitchen table with a pen: *Dear Jonathan* . . .

Chapter Sixteen

Ryan met me in the hotel lobby about four thirty the next night.

"Are we going in style?" I asked.

He beamed, seeming almost as excited as I was. "Will a Hummer work?"

"Sounds perfect. Is Erica waiting out there?"

"Not exactly," Ryan said. "She called and asked me to pick her up out at Mercy's."

I couldn't imagine why Erica would have gone to Mercy's house early, especially since it would mean that she would have to leave her car there while we were at the restaurant. Maybe she thought Mercy would be more at ease if she were there alone. If so, I was 100 percent in favor of it. Whatever it took to draw Mercy out was fine with me.

"Let's go then," I said.

I climbed into the back of the Hummer, and we were on our way to Mercy's.

I couldn't wait to see Mercy's face when she saw how we were going to get to the restaurant. I was certain she had never been in something quite like this before. I almost felt like a kid on Christmas Day watching someone open a present he had worked especially hard on. Funny thing was, I couldn't understand why I felt such a kinship with Mercy. My best guess was that it was because she had been an abandoned child, like I was.

Mercy had had a difficult life, and I could not change that. But I could treat her to a special night out—one she would not forget.

The temperature was dropping fast, now that the sun had gone down. The weather reports said it could drop to thirty or more below. Not a great night for a date, but we did not have much choice.

I sincerely hoped this would be my last night in Fairbanks.

I did not know how much information Mercy would be able—or willing—to give me, but whatever it was, it would have to do. I needed to get back to my company, and quite frankly, I didn't care anymore if Tim agreed or not.

At least I found out that Ada Guthrie had not given me up because of something I had done. As far as I was concerned, it wasn't necessary to dig much deeper into her motives.

I was ready to go home. Fairbanks was a place of memories. A few good ones, but most of them were bad. Only time would tell whether digging up my past would help me deal with my anger. One thing was certain. If Mercy didn't have anything more to tell me, I was done.

There was one person, however, whom I would miss when I left: Erica. She definitely earned a spot on the short list of reporters I liked. And, amazingly, she took it a step further. After my last marriage broke up, I decided not to get

married again. I didn't even want to date. If I was that difficult to be around, if I was such a toxic person, perhaps it was
better for me to remain a bachelor.

I had gotten used to living on my own, and although I
missed the companionship a little, I felt I could be happy living by myself.

Erica was the first woman who had made me question
that decision. I enjoyed her company and wanted to be
around her more. But she didn't appear to be interested in
working for the *Miami Herald*, and I was definitely not moving
to Fairbanks.

Of course, that didn't mean I couldn't come up and
visit—in the summer. The last few days of Alaska's winter
weather were enough to last me a lifetime.

Ryan turned the limo down Mercy's road. There was no
way the big Hummer could navigate her driveway, and even
if it could get down there, Ryan wouldn't have room to turn
it around. So he pulled to the side of the road, and I walked
down to get Ada and Erica.

When I stepped out of the limo, I instantly realized that
the weather reports had not been exaggerated. The cold air
blasted my face and burned the inside of my nostrils.

As I got closer to Mercy's cabin, I thought of my current
attire and chuckled. Long underwear, Carhartts, a heavy
flannel shirt, fur-lined mittens and parka, a ski mask, and
bunny boots were not exactly the style I was used to display-
ing on a date. I was more the gold cufflinks and Italian loafers
type. But since I didn't relish a case of frostbite, fashion had
to be relegated to the back burner.

I knocked on Mercy's door, expecting to be greeted by the now-familiar barking of her dog, but this time all was silent. I was beginning to think nobody was there when I finally heard Erica's voice.

"Just a minute," she called.

"Better be less than that," I yelled back. "Another minute out here and I might be a Popsicle."

Seconds later the door opened and Erica motioned me inside.

"Why isn't the pooch making a fuss?" I asked.

Erica closed the door. "We took him to a neighbor's this afternoon."

"Why?"

Erica shrugged. "Mercy was afraid the dog might try to bite you."

"Speaking of Mercy, where is she?"

"Back in her bedroom. We have something to show you. Have a seat." Erica motioned toward the sofa as she turned to go down the hallway. "And close your eyes," she said.

"Aren't we being a little dramatic?" I called after her.

"Uh-uh. Close 'em."

I sat down and closed my eyes. "Okay," I said. "They're closed."

I heard Erica say to Mercy, "Come on out."

A few seconds later I heard their footsteps entering the living room. "You can open them now," Erica said.

When I opened my eyes, I couldn't believe that the woman who stood before me was the same Mercy I had talked to yesterday. Her black hair was no longer dull and matted. It had been washed and styled beautifully. And she wore makeup that took years off her appearance. But even more than that, Mercy's smile was radiant. If it were possible, I would have said she was glowing.

She was also wearing new clothes. Not a dress—thirty below is not dress weather. But she wore an attractive blue pant suit, accented by a faux pearl necklace.

In a word, the change in Mercy was stunning.

"Mercy, you look lovely," I said. "I just wish I'd bought you a corsage."

"Thought of that," Erica said, handing me a plastic container that held a corsage made from three red roses.

"I owe you one," I said. Then I pinned the corsage on Mercy and held out my arm. "I'd be honored if you'd accompany me to dinner."

Mercy blushed and looked away.

A few minutes later we were all bundled up and headed out to the Hummer. The wind had picked up, making the air all the more piercing.

"I need to bring my car back into town," Erica said. "I'll meet you at the restaurant."

"Are you sure?" I asked. "How often do you get a chance to ride in one of these?"

Erica laughed. "I'll hitch a ride when we bring Mercy home."

I helped Mercy up her driveway and into the Hummer. "Have you ever had a ride like this before?" I asked.

She shook her head, beaming as she looked around.

"I hope this will be a special evening for you. One you'll remember for a long time."

"Thank you," she said in a quiet voice.

I turned off the interior light so we could see the lights of Fairbanks as we drove back toward the town. I knew that Erica would not approve of me starting to question Mercy so soon, but I felt it couldn't hurt to get the ball rolling a little early.

"You know, we have a lot in common," I said.

Mercy didn't respond, so I continued.

"Well, we were both born in Fairbanks, weren't we? I moved away, and you stayed here your whole life, but we're both native Alaskans."

Mercy nodded.

"You know what one of my favorite memories of Alaska is?"

"What?" she asked timidly.

"It's one of the only things I remember that my mother and I did together. The summer I was four years old, she took me to Pioneer Park. Of course, back then it was called Alaskaland. I don't remember a whole lot about that day, but I do remember riding the train around the park.

"It was a bright, warm summer day, and we must have ridden that train ten times. I kept dragging her back there again and again. Almost everything else about that day is fuzzy," I said.

"I do remember one other detail, though. She took me around and showed me all the old cabins and told me how they weren't fake. They were real cabins that people had actually lived in. Then she took me to one of the cabins and told me that it had been her home when she was a little girl. I thought that was pretty amazing.

"Funny, but I didn't remember any of that until I drove by the park the other day. I've been too busy, but I wish I'd had the time to go by there. I bet I'd remember the cabin if I saw it again. Unfortunately, I'll be flying back to Miami tomorrow if I can wrap up my business here tonight. Of course, you know you're a big part of that."

Mercy nodded.

"I told you why I was up here, didn't I?"

"You want to know about Ada," she said.

"That's right. And that's the other thing we have in common. You said that you don't remember your father. That he left your mother when you were very young?"

"Uh-huh," said Mercy.

"Well, the same thing happened to me. My father left Ada before I was born. They say you can't miss what you never had. It must be true because I don't miss my father. But it wasn't just him. When I was four years old, not long after my mother took me to Alaskaland, she put me up for adoption, and I never saw her again.

"And that's why I'm up here. I'm trying to find out why Ada did what she did. I'm trying to understand. Since you knew her, I'm hoping you might be able to tell me something that might help me. Do you think you could do that?"

There was a long pause before Mercy answered. "Maybe."

"Maybe?" I said. "Maybe you know something, or maybe you'll be willing to help me?"

Her answer was quiet but unmistakable: "Maybe I'll be willing to help."

I was on familiar turf now. Mercy wanted to negotiate. If

the price was right, she would help me. Now all I had to do was figure out what that price would be."

"What would you like? I'll do whatever it takes."

Mercy didn't answer.

"Do you want a brand-new house with indoor plumbing? Maybe a car so you don't have to take the bus everywhere? Name it, and it's yours."

Mercy mumbled something, but I could only make out the name "Ada."

"What was that? You want me to do something about Ada?"

Mercy looked at the floor, and her voice was barely audible. "Forgive Ada."

I sat there, stunned. Then I laughed. I wasn't making fun of her. It's just that her request was preposterous.

"Forgive Ada? Why would you ask for something like that?"

"Your mama loved you," Mercy replied. "That's what Ada would want me to ask for."

"And if I say no?"

Mercy looked down and shook her head.

I sat silently for a moment, trying to collect my thoughts. This timid little lady who lived in a dry cabin in Alaska just did something that many tough businessmen had been unable to do. She had bested me in a negotiation. She had asked for the one thing I couldn't give.

"We're there," Ryan said. He turned off the road and pulled up to the restaurant's front door.

I looked over at Mercy. I knew I shouldn't be angry with her, but I was. "She loved me?" I asked. "Well, she had a strange way of showing it." I continued, my voice rising, "I've lived my whole life with the pain she caused me. Let me tell you something, Mercy. As long as I live, I'll never forgive Ada for what she did."

I regretted those words the second they came out of my mouth, but it was too late.

Tears filled Mercy's eyes, and she started to tremble.

Ryan opened her door, and she climbed out of the Hummer. Erica was standing beside Ryan and said, "Well, did you have a good ri—" But Mercy brushed past her, crying.

Erica looked in at me. "What happened? Did you say something to her?"

"I lost my temper."

Erica turned and ran after Mercy, but before she did, she gave me a look of disappointment mixed with contempt.

Once again, I had turned toxic.

Once again, I had left casualties in my wake.

My BlackBerry rang about thirty minutes later. Ryan and I were sitting at a table in the restaurant, waiting for Erica to bring Mercy back.

"Hello?"

"What did you say to her?" Erica sounded furious.

"I don't think it's what I said as much as how I said it."

"I don't care what it is," she said. "How could you raise your voice to that sweet lady? You need to get out there and apologize to her right now."

"Where is she?"

"I took her home. She didn't want to come back to the restaurant, and I don't blame her."

Now it was my turn to accuse. "You left her there by herself?"

Erica's tone was not at all defensive. "This is not about me, buster. It's about you. She wouldn't let me stay with her, or I'd still be out there. Now make it right!"

She hung up before I could answer.

Ryan was trying to look nonchalant, as if he hadn't heard the conversation. Erica had been yelling so loud, I wouldn't have been surprised if everybody in the restaurant had heard it.

"Can you take me back out there?" I asked.

"Sure, but do you really want to go in the Hummer?"

I shook my head. "No. Get me something small and humble."

It fit my mood. I was feeling pretty small at the moment.

We drove by the limo service and switched the Hummer for the Jeep we had been driving earlier in the week; then we headed out toward Mercy's place.

The instant we pulled into her driveway, I knew something was wrong.

All the lights were out. The place looked deserted.

"Point the Jeep so the headlights hit the front door," I said.

The door was open.

Ryan and I jumped out of the Jeep and ran over to the little house. "Mercy? Mercy, are you okay?"

Nobody answered.

"Check the house," I told him. "I'll get the other buildings."

I ran around back and checked the out buildings. They were dark and cold and empty. By the time I made my way back to the front door, Ryan was coming out and closing it behind him. He shook his head.

"She can't have gone far, not in this weather," I said. "Let's check the road."

We hopped back in the Jeep and drove up and down Mercy's road. "Take it slow," I said. I pulled out my BlackBerry and called Erica. It rang once, twice, three times.

"Come on, Erica. This isn't the time to start ignoring me."

She picked up on the sixth ring.

"Did you apologize?"

"Don't hang up," I said. "Something's wrong. Mercy's not here. Her house is dark, and the front door was open. We're checking up and down the road, but so far we don't see anything."

"She wouldn't just walk away," Erica said. "She's lived here long enough to know that she'd never last."

Unless she doesn't care about that.

I hated that thought, but as distraught as Mercy was when she left me, it was certainly a possibility. Before I could voice the thought, Erica broke in with a suggestion.

"Check the bus stop at Ski Boot Hill Road. The buses run until six thirty. She could be waiting for the Gray Line.

If she's not there, then check the transit stations. She might be trying to connect to another route."

"But where could she be going?" I asked.

"Not far, that's for sure. Most of the bus lines will only take her around Fairbanks, so she can't be going far. The Green Line will take her down to North Pole, but that's only about fifteen miles. While you're doing that, I'll see if I can get the police to help look for her."

"You don't think they'll help?"

"If she were a child, sure. But Mercy is an adult and has been missing less than an hour. They're probably going to think we're overreacting. But I have some friends on the force. I'll see what I can do."

After I hung up, I told Ryan to swing by the Gray Line bus stop at Ski Boot Hill and Farmers Loop. Nobody was there.

"Well, if she was waiting for a bus, she already caught it," Ryan said.

"Take me back to her house," I said. "Then I want you to check the transit stations to see if she's trying to make a connection to another line. Be sure and check the Green Line. North Pole isn't all that far away, but if she's trying to run away, that might be far enough for her."

"Why do you want to go back to her cabin?" asked Ryan.

"I want to see if there's anything that might help us figure out where she is. Once you've made the rounds of the transit stations, come back and pick me up."

Mercy's house was dark and bitterly cold. The fire in her wood stove had burned down to almost nothing, and the frigid night air blowing through the front door removed any heat that had built up in the little cabin.

After I closed the door behind me, I turned on a table lamp and put a few logs into the stove. When we brought Mercy home, I wanted it to be warm.

It was the least I could do.

Ryan probably wouldn't take long to make a sweep of the transit stations, so I didn't have a lot of time to work. The problem was, I didn't know what I was looking for. I looked around the living room, but there wasn't much aside from the furniture and a few old magazines on the coffee table.

I looked in all her kitchen drawers but again found nothing other than what you would expect to find in anybody's kitchen. There were no papers or bills or address books. For the first time I noticed that there wasn't even a phone.

On my way down the hall, I passed by the dog's bowls. On the front of one bowl was the dog's name, Tundra, in crudely painted letters.

I opened Mercy's bedroom door and flipped on the light.

The bedroom was as spartan as the rest of the house. Against the far wall was a single bed covered by a homemade patchwork quilt. If Mercy had made it herself, she was quite skilled. It was a beautiful piece of work.

A small desk sat just inside the door to my right. An old scrapbook lay on top of the desk. The title on the cover: *Memories*.

Four color photos, grainy and faded, were taped to the first page. They were of a smiling—and much younger—Mercy, lying in a hospital bed and holding a baby. There were several more pictures of Mercy and her child on the next page, but one in particular caught my eye.

Mercy and a little boy were standing outside one of the cabins in Pioneer Park's Gold Rush Town.

The picture caught my eye because I was the little boy.

A caption under the picture read, "One last good time together."

I took the scrapbook over to the bed and sat down. There were no more photos after the second page, but the scrapbook was filled with newspaper and magazine clippings about me. Mercy had chronicled every major achievement in my life—and most of the minor ones—since I had become a public figure.

Many pages had little notes with smiley faces or hearts. All of the notes expressed the same idea. She was proud of me.

I leafed through the whole book and was equally amazed at what was not there. In recent years, particularly, I have had my share of bad press and graced the front page of plenty of tabloids. My marital troubles, painkiller addiction, suicide attempt, and rehab had been fodder for the scandal-hungry media.

Mercy had not saved a single negative article.

Not one.

Tucked inside the back cover was an envelope, sealed, and with a handwritten name on it.

My stomach tightened as I read the name: Jonathan.

I opened it and began to read.

Chapter Seventeen

Dearest Jonathan,

There are so many things I would like to say to you, but it's hard for me to talk to people, and I don't think I could ever say these things face-to-face. So I thought that maybe if I wrote you a letter, it would work better. I don't know if I'll ever have the courage to send it to you, but maybe I can give it to your friend Erica.

I am so proud of you. Even though I have been out of your life since you were four, I have watched you. Sometimes that got me into trouble, but I just couldn't help myself. I'm as proud of you as any mother could ever be.

There were so many times that I wanted to pick you up and hold you, but I gave up that right a long time ago. It's not something I am proud of. And I wish I could say I had a good reason for giving you up.

Your daddy walked out on me when I was expecting you. He lied to me and hurt me deeper than I've ever been hurt, before or since. I know I should have forgiven him, but I didn't.

I decided that I was going to raise you myself, but that was harder than I thought it would be. I tried for a while, but the older you got the more you looked like your daddy.

Every time I looked at you, I remembered what he did to me, and I got angry.

One day I almost hit you.

That was when I decided that no matter how much I loved you, I had to give you up 'cause the last thing I ever wanted to do was hurt you.

Maybe putting you up for adoption wasn't the right thing to do. I can tell you that a day hasn't gone by that I haven't felt ashamed.

The other day, I lied about my name because I didn't want you to know who I was. Since you thought you were talking to my neighbor, not to me, I just let you keep thinking that. My house burned down a few years ago and I moved in with my elderly neighbor. She didn't have any family either, and she left this house to me when she died.

I told you my name was Mercy. That comes from my favorite hymn. It reminds me that even if nobody else forgives me, God does because of his son, Jesus.

Once the weather is better, and as soon as I can figure out where, I'm going to move away. Probably somewhere deeper into the interior. Now that you're moving your business to Fairbanks, I don't think I can stand to see you around town so often.

I am looking forward to our dinner tonight. It will be one last good time together even though you won't know who I am. But that's okay because it's the only way I could do it.

I hope someday you'll forgive me for what I did. I know I don't deserve it.

I will always love you,
Ada

Chapter Eighteen

I sat there, gripping the letter in stunned silence and trying to hold myself together emotionally. For so many years, the only emotion I'd felt was anger. But at that moment, all I wanted to do was dissolve into tears.

But that wouldn't help Ada.

She was out there somewhere, and if she wasn't inside a building or some kind of shelter, she had very little time to live.

I heard a horn honk outside. Ryan was back.

It was a long shot, but there was only one connection that I could think of. A couple of the last lines of Ada's letter read: "I am looking forward to our dinner tonight. It will be one last good time together even though you won't know who I am."

The caption underneath the picture of Ada and me also read: "One last good time together."

I ran out to the Jeep.

"I think I know where she is," I said. "Head to Pioneer Park."

As Ryan drove, I dialed Erica.

"Are the police going to help?" I asked.

"Yes, but they can't canvass the whole city," she said.

"Have them check Gold Rush Town in Pioneer Park. It's the last place we went together when I was four."

Erica sounded dumbfounded. "The last place—when you were four? What?"

"I'll explain later. Just get them there. We're on our way."

The drive from Ada's house to Pioneer Park was short, only a few miles that took us about fifteen minutes, but for me it was torturously long. On that long ride I felt as if every hateful thought I had ever had about this woman replayed in my mind.

For the first time, I saw unmasked the destructive power of my unwillingness to forgive. And I felt the terrible consequences.

By the time we turned in to Pioneer Park, I saw red and blue flashing lights in the direction of Gold Rush Town. Erica was standing by an ambulance, talking to a police officer. Ryan parked the Jeep, and I ran over to the ambulance.

The EMTs were loading Ada into the back of the vehicle just as I got there.

She wasn't moving.

"Is she okay?" I asked.

They slammed the doors closed without a word, and the ambulance drove off with its siren blaring.

I turned to Erica. "Is she okay?"

I couldn't read the expression on her face.

"She was unconscious when they got here, but she's still alive. She's got some frostbite. Beyond that, I don't know."

"Will you ride to the hospital with me?" I asked.

Erica nodded. "Let's go."

Fairbanks Memorial was not far from the park, and we arrived there in less than ten minutes.

They already had Ada in the treatment room, so all we could do was sit and wait.

Erica sat in a chair beside me. "What did you mean about you and Mercy going to Pioneer Park when you were four?"

"Mercy is my mother. She is Ada Guthrie. She's been following me all my life. There's a scrapbook at her place filled with articles and news clippings about me. She also has a handful of pictures from when I was a baby. The last picture was taken at Pioneer Park, just before she put me up for adoption."

"But why didn't she tell us?"

I shrugged. "She was afraid, ashamed, embarrassed."

"What did you say to her that got her so upset?"

I leaned forward and rested my head in my hands. "I think she was about to open up and tell me who she really was. But she said that she'd only tell me if I promised to forgive Ada for what she'd done. I lost my cool and told her that as long as I lived, I'd never forgive my mother for abandoning me. I'm sorry. I'd do anything to take those words back."

At that moment the waiting room door opened, and a young doctor came in. She looked around the room and said, "Ada Guthrie?"

I raised my hand and stood up. "Over here. How is she?"

"She has some minor frostbite, but she'll be fine. We're going to keep her overnight just to be on the safe side, but she can go home tomorrow. Would you like to go back and see her before she goes up to a room?"

"Maybe you'd better go first," I said to Erica. "I don't want to upset her any further. If she tells you that she wants to see me, then I'll go back."

Erica followed the doctor to the treatment room. While I was waiting, I went over to the receptionist to take care of Ada's paperwork.

When the receptionist asked about my relationship to the patient, I said something I never thought I would say.

"She's my mother."

About ten minutes later, Erica came back from the treatment room, carrying the rose corsage. I wondered whether Ada would be willing to see me, but Erica's expression didn't inspire hope. Then she shook her head and handed me the corsage.

"It's a no, I guess," I said.

"When I mentioned the possibility of you coming back there, she fell apart. It took quite a while just to get her calmed down again."

I was disappointed but not surprised. I had been pretty harsh the last time we were together.

"I wonder whether she'll ever forgive me," I said.

"I don't think that's the issue right now," Erica said. "She's not mad at you. She is so ashamed, she can't face you. She needs to know that you forgive her. Then you can work on asking her to forgive you," Erica added.

"But how can I do that if she won't even talk to me?"

"I don't know," Erica said.

"Will you stay here with her? At least till she gets settled in her room? I'll make sure Ryan's available to take you back to your car whenever you need to go."

"Sure," she said. "What are you going to do?"

"Go back to my hotel room and try to figure out how to tear down a wall I've spent half my life building."

Most of the evening I wrestled with my thoughts. I tried to pray, but I felt that my prayers were bouncing off the ceiling. I don't know exactly what I expected. Maybe I thought God would drop a solution in my lap. If that was the case, nothing was coming.

Finally, I decided to call the man who was responsible for me being up here in the first place. I hated to wake him up—it would be almost two in the morning in Miami—but Tim had sent me on this mission and I desperately needed his advice on how to finish it.

I hit speed dial on my BlackBerry. It took a few rings before Tim picked up.

"Jonathan, what's up?" Tim asked.

He was trying to sound like I hadn't gotten him out of bed, but I knew better.

I plopped down in the big leather recliner and put my feet up. Then I explained everything that had happened. As I finished, I said, "I need a little wisdom."

"Sounds to me like you're doing great," Tim said. "You're right where you need to be."

"What do you mean?"

"You've been bitter toward your mother your entire life. Now you have the opportunity to let go of that."

"I know that," I said. "But how can you forgive someone who won't even talk to you?"

"Words are important, but they can be overrated. It's easy to repeat the words 'I forgive you' and not mean a thing. Find a way to show her."

"But how?"

"How did God show you that he loved you?"

"He sent his son to die for me, but—"

"Grace, my friend. Show her grace."

"Yeah, but how do I do that?"

"You'll know," Tim said before he disconnected.

I sat there a long time, pondering Tim's words. I had brought Ada's scrapbook and letter with me. I leafed through the scrapbook, looking at the articles and the notes she had written by each. I kept coming back to the picture of us at Pioneer Park and the caption: "One last good time together."

That was in her letter too: "I am looking forward to our dinner tonight. It will be one last good time together."

Over on the desk sat Ada's rose corsage, a little battered and wilted but still beautiful.

"I am looking forward to our dinner."

Tim's voice echoed in my mind: *Show her grace.*

I punched in Erica's number. When she picked up, I said, "I think I know what to do, but I need your help."

"If it will help Ada, I'll do anything."

"I need you to pick up Ada when they discharge her tomorrow and then bring her here to the hotel. I'll arrange for a room in her name. Tomorrow night about six, bring her down to the restaurant and get a table as far away from the front entrance as you can. Once you're settled in, I'll call you. Excuse yourself and tell her that you need to take the call in private. I'll take it from there."

<hr>

I glanced at my watch. It was almost 6:00 p.m., and it had been one of the longest days of my life. I felt terrified. I had no idea if what I had planned would work.

Erica had called me after she checked Ada into her room. She wasn't sure how well things were going to go. Ada had become depressed and withdrawn. Erica almost hadn't been able to get her to come to the hotel. She had to get the doctors to tell Ada that a few days in a hotel would be a good idea before she went back to her cabin. Even then, Ada was hesitant to come, but when Erica told her that the room and all her meals were free, she agreed.

Thankfully, she didn't ask who was paying for everything. If she had, she might not have come.

Now, if Erica could get her to the restaurant, we would be in business.

I felt like a teenage boy going to his first prom.

I dressed in the outfit I liked to wear for a night on the town: a navy blue blazer with gold buttons, matching dress slacks, and my Italian loafers. Definitely not the right kind of clothing for Alaskan winter weather, but I wasn't planning on going outside.

Earlier in the day I had gone to the barber and gotten a haircut and shave.

I retrieved Ada's corsage from the refrigerator and took a deep breath. Then I called Erica.

"Are you both down there?"

"Uh-huh," she said.

"Okay, I've got it from here."

I took the elevator down to the lobby. The closer I got to the restaurant, the more my heart felt as if it were in my throat.

I asked for a table near the front entrance.

From my table, I could see Ada, but she hadn't seen me.

I felt like crying. The beautiful, glowing woman from the previous night was nowhere to be seen. Her hair was matted again, and instead of a nice outfit, she wore a tattered old coat and an ugly scarf.

Her eyes reflected such deep sadness, it couldn't be measured.

She sat there, hunched and defensive, like someone who's been beaten down so many times she couldn't will herself to get back up.

I looked around and waved the wine steward over to my table.

"May I help you, sir?"

"Yes. What's the best wine you have?"

"We have a nice 2005 Quilceda Creek Cabernet. Two hundred dollars a bottle."

"That sounds great."

He broke into a big smile. "Very good. I'll be back in a moment."

A few minutes later he came back with the wine. He showed me the label, then pulled the cork and showed it to me. I nodded, and he poured a little into a glass and handed it to me.

I swirled it in the glass, taking in the deep red color and inhaling the aroma, then I took a sip and swished it around in my mouth. I nodded to the steward, and he filled my glass.

"Would you do me a favor?" I asked.

"Certainly."

"Would you take a glass to the lady at that table across the room? And would you give her this message for me?"

He smiled as I whispered my message into his ear.

Chapter Nineteen

Ada was nervous. Erica had to answer a phone call, but she should have been back a long time ago. Ada couldn't understand what was taking so long.

She had finally decided to give up and go back to her room when she saw Jonathan sitting at a table near the front door. If she tried to leave now, she would have to walk right past his table. She had done exactly that a few days ago, but it was different then. Jonathan hadn't known who she was, and she had been able to pass by him unnoticed. She was even able to turn back and look at him while he read his paper.

If he was sitting anywhere else, Ada would have run from the restaurant. She just prayed that he hadn't seen her.

Ada shifted her seat and looked in a different direction. She thought about moving to another chair and facing away from Jonathan, but then she saw him talking to a man and pointing at her table. What was he doing?

The man poured a glass of wine and started walking in her direction.

Ada watched, helpless, as the man brought the glass of

wine to her table. He set the glass down in front of her and motioned toward Jonathan.

"The gentleman across the room sends this with his compliments."

Ada gazed down at the glass of wine, not sure of what to do or say.

"He also sends a message. He asked me to tell you that he loves you and that he's proud to call you his mother."

The wine glass blurred.

Ada blinked, and a teardrop fell onto the white table-cloth. She watched it glisten briefly in the soft light and then soak into the cloth.

"He also asked if he might have the pleasure of dining with you tonight."

Ada brushed away the tears with the backs of her hands. She looked up to answer the man, but he had left. She turned and glanced back at Jonathan's table. He sat there with his wine glass in his hand.

Ada picked up her glass, and it trembled in her hand.

She raised her glass.

Jonathan smiled and raised his.

Then he stood and walked over to her table. As he came toward her, Ada felt years of shame evaporate like a fog disappearing in the hot morning sun.

Jonathan—her son—stood beside her table and handed her a corsage.

She would treasure his next four words for the rest of her life.

"I love you, Mother."

Chapter Twenty

How do you tear down a wall you've been building most of your life?

One brick at a time.

That dinner marked a new beginning for both of us. We still had plenty of issues to work through, but whatever they were, we would handle them together. Ada was disappointed to learn that the stories about me moving my company to Fairbanks were only rumors. And over the next few days she did her best to convince me that I should turn those rumors into reality. I told her that no matter how much I loved her, I was too used to living in a warm weather climate to move back to Alaska. Then I turned the tables on her and tried to talk her into moving to Miami.

She wouldn't budge. She loves Alaska as much as I love Florida. Even though she wasn't willing to move, I convinced her to let me buy her a house with heat and indoor plumbing.

One thing was certain. I planned to make a lot more trips to Fairbanks in the coming months and years. We had a lot of lost time to catch up on.

And I had a second reason to visit Fairbanks.

Erica had officially made the list of reporters I liked. And I made her top-ten list of Fortune 500 CEOs. We decided that we needed to talk more.

A lot more.

I might even grant her that interview. And who knows? Maybe I will give some thought to opening a branch office up there.

And I have a new favorite hymn now. My mother taught it to me:

> There's a wideness in God's mercy
> Like the wideness of the sea;
> There's a kindness in his justice,
> Which is more than liberty.
> There is welcome for the sinner,
> And more graces for the good;
> There is mercy with the Savior;
> There is healing in his blood.
> For the love of God is broader
> Than the measure of man's mind;
> And the heart of the Eternal
> Is most wonderfully kind.

The Truth Behind the Fiction

I hope you have enjoyed reading *The Encounter*. What you have just experienced is a fictional account based on two true stories combined into one. Each of the situations was as dramatic and profound to me as the fictional story. I have written those true accounts below and have some questions and concepts for you to consider after reading.

—Stephen Arterburn

History Repeated

It was in the late 1990s that I conducted an intensive program for people who wanted to change their lives. Whether it was overeating or depression or shame, we had a group for those who wanted to find a new and different way to live. Participants showed up at a retreat center in San Juan Capistrano, California, where there were beauty and solitude and not much else to do other than focus on their own issues, addictions, or ruts they had dug into.

I spoke ten times or so over a four-day period, and in

between each session the participants attended a group therapy session with a licensed clinical therapist. It was a powerful format. Often people said that they revealed more, worked through more, and healed more than they had in months or years of going to see a counselor. Then when they returned to that counselor, their work was much more effective and useful.

The success of these programs continues today in a modified program that takes place over a three-day weekend. Rather than conduct them in Southern California, we take them all over the country to a different city each time. You can find out about these New Life weekends at newlife.com.

So it was in the late 1990s that I was conducting one of these intensive weekends when a very distraught man came up to me before a session started. He asked if he could speak with me, so I asked him what was wrong. He told me that for a lifetime he had hated the mother he never knew. He did not know her because when he was an infant, she had dropped him off at a neighbor's house and he never saw her again. She had become bad in every way in his mind, but he thought that he had outgrown any issues he had with her.

He was upset because she found a way to get in touch with him and asked if she could see him. She wanted to talk about her life and his and the future. He did not know what to say. He was so angry that she had left him behind, but he was able to contain himself during the call. He told her he would need some time. Then he took her number and said he would call her back.

His question for me was, "What should I do?"

I talked to him for a while and ascertained some details of his life. Anger was his biggest problem, and his rage started with this woman he had never known. He felt insulted that she wanted to be part of his life after he had survived into adulthood. She was not there when he needed her, and he did not want to be there now that she needed him. So he was angry and confused and in need of direction to make sense of it all.

There are times when you just need the right words for a specific situation, and when they come, you believe they came from somewhere other than you. That was the case when I talked with this man. On that day, for some supernatural reason, I had the right words for the situation. I suggested that he call his mother and ask her one question before he decided whether to let her into his life: What was her childhood like? I knew it couldn't be too pretty, but it was still like a shot in the dark. He said he was willing to do it after the session that night. I did not see him the rest of the evening.

The next morning, before the first session started, he came up to me, and he looked like an entirely different person. He was calm, and he had a grin on his face. He asked me if I was a prophet. I said, "Do you mean prophet or fortune-teller?" He replied, "I don't know what you call it, but somehow you knew I needed to know about her childhood."

Naturally, I asked him, "Well, what did you find out?"

He responded with the following story: "I found out that she and I had something very important in common. I found out that her mother, my grandmother, was a very disturbed woman who sank into a deep depression after having each of her children. The depression would be easy enough to endure, but she also had fits of rage. In her rage, my grandmother had hit my mother and then realized that if something did not change, she might end up severely hurting or killing her. So my grandmother did to my mother what my mother did to me. My mother was abandoned as a small child to be raised by the neighbors.

"She then explained that she had heard the story from an aunt, my grandmother's sister. My grandmother did what she could do to protect my mom, and the only thing she knew to do was to have someone else raise her.

"My mother became pregnant with me in her early twenties, and after my birth, she sank into a severe postpartum depression. She did not know the term back then, but she felt some of the urges her mother had probably felt. She never hit me, but it was all she could do to control herself. After days of fighting the urges, she knew she had to protect me. So she took me next door, left me on the doorstep, and left to live on the street, in shelters for a while and eventually in a halfway house. Part of her recovery was making amends with me, so she wanted to see me in person to do it.

"So you see, the thing she did that caused me to hate her was the only thing she knew she could do to protect me. She was not cruel to me. She was trying to save my life and keep me safe."

Well, as I said, sometimes you just have the right words to say for the right occasion. The words that led him to call the woman he hated make a very important point for those who want to live their lives in the truth. Sometimes, people have a story. But it is not the real story. And often it is not even close to the real story. And often that real story imagines a person as more wonderfully good than anyone can possibly be or just the opposite. In the case of this man, he had made his mother out to be all bad, even cruel. But that was not the case.

Learning the truth changed his life, and he went on to establish a relationship with his mother that was pretty remarkable. He stayed in touch with me for a while but soon moved on to e-mailing someone other than me. But while we were in contact he was glad to be in relationship with his mother. It had filled a large hole in his life. I suspect the relationship continues.

Perhaps you have filled your life with anger or even hatred for another person. Perhaps the person is someone you have never even met. Maybe you have a story that is not the real story. It might be time for you to do a little research, asking brothers and sisters, aunts and uncles, or anyone who might have been there when you were young. Again and again I find people astonished at how different reality is from the reality they have created in their minds. Or the reverse could happen. Someone you idealized might turn out to be something other than the angel you imagined. The idealization may have prevented you from having to deal with all of the dimensions of pain and disappointment you would have to confront and manage if you looked at the truth about the past.

Getting Past the Past

No matter what you discover about your past, it most likely calls for forgiveness in order for resolution to happen. To maintain resentment robs you of the life God has for you. Resentment prevents you from moving on, reminding you of the past as if it were yesterday. Making the past the past is the goal.

There are those who suggest that it is a mistake to deal with the past. We should just move on. We are new creations, instantly transformed, so there is nothing that the past has to do with the present. When I hear this advice, I wonder whether the speaker actually believes it. But let's say it was true, that you should not spend your time dealing with the past that cannot be changed. You still must deal with what is hampering your present, and if something from the past continues to crop up as a source of shame or anger or fear, it really is not the past. If it is creeping into today, it needs to be dealt with.

Dealing with It

Dealing with it means taking action that will heal and resolve and allow you to be free. There are several elements of dealing with whatever it was in your past that has made an imprint on who you are today. There is the element of truth and the need to discover it. Once uncovered there may be a need to grieve. You may need to grieve the loss of the parent you thought you had in order to accept and forgive the one you do have.

Grieving is a combination of experiencing the anger and sadness in a way that when it is done, the event or the knowledge of the event does not hurt like it did when it happened. To experience grief in a helpful way, you most likely need to talk with another person who is willing to listen to you and accept the feelings you need to express. The person does not have to be a trained professional.

Knowing the truth, forgiving, and grieving lead to an important concept in healing: acceptance. You may deny the reality of your life or the reality of your past. Maybe it is just too painful to accept that alcohol has become the controlling factor in your life. Or maybe you cannot accept that you are the controlling factor in a marriage that is being controlled to its death. When you stop denying and rationalizing, you can begin the process of acceptance.

Acceptance means that it does not matter how you arrived at the current situation; it is your situation to handle. Yes, someone else may have hurt you badly. Yes, someone may have neglected you or held you up so high as a favorite that the rest of life has been a disappointment. And some of you have been badly abused in every way unimaginable. Any of these situations are reasons to hate and fear and live in shame. But you have to go beyond the entitlement of resentment so you can have the freedom found in acceptance.

All teenagers have to confront hurtful things. For me it was rejection. I felt it from some kids whose dads made more money than mine. And I felt it from friends who did not consider me enough of a friend to include me on an annual trip. At first I was confused about why. Then I was angry. Then

I accepted the truth. The truth was that my friends' parents were also going with my fifteen-year-old friends. And on that annual trip there was a lot of drinking by the parents. My parents did not drink, so they were not on the list of invitees either. Discovering that piece of information about their non-drinking stance helped me accept the reality of the situation.

The reality was that it had nothing to do with me. It had everything to do with my parents, who had character and were not given to times of drunkenness on a trip with their kids. Not going made me sad, but accepting the real reason made it easier. It was not a rejection of me personally but a rejection of a way of life that our family had chosen. Rather than be angry, I was a little proud that our family stood for something. It helped me find acceptance and helped me move on rather than be stuck in harsh feelings of rejection and abandonment.

When I have dealt with couples in trouble, the issue is often a lack of acceptance. Perhaps he is unwilling to accept that his sexual impulses are not normal. Maybe he rejects the thought of being a sex addict even though he has used pornography extensively and had many affairs. He rejects the truth because he cannot imagine surviving without his lust to energize him and make him feel like a man.

His wife may have an acceptance problem also. She wants to believe that if she loves him a little more or better, he will change. Or perhaps she believes that God will change him, and it is her mission to hang in there until God does. Most likely nothing good is going to happen until she accepts reality. Not the reality of his immorality. That is obvious. But she must come to accept that she is wishing things will get better and doing nothing because she is so afraid. Acceptance will lead her to determine that the only way things will change is for her to make a bold move and require him to get help. Acceptance is not easy, but it is a must if you want to live effectively in reality.

Making Amends

The entire emotional trauma was dug up when a mother wanted to make amends. She wanted to try to make it right with her son. She wanted to tell him she was sorry she missed his life, and she wanted to ask for his forgiveness. Then she was hopeful she could live out her amends by being in his life and giving him the love she had been unable to express.

Too often we sit around and wait for someone to make things right with us when we are the ones who need to move to right a wrong. When someone attempts to make amends, it is easy to reject that person, but accepting the effort to right the wrong helps that person and it helps you more. It allows you to bring closure to a festering wound. All of us truly need to be slow to anger and quick to forgive and restore.

The Second True Story: Alaska

In the early 1980s I worked for a publicly traded health care company called Comprehensive Care Corporation (known as CompCare). Compcare was a very successful company providing psychiatric care, and it was becoming the largest provider of alcoholism treatment in the country. The alcohol treatment units were called CareUnits, and they were managed by CompCare in Medical Surgical Hospitals, which had a contract with the company.

Not only did I oversee one-third of the country, but I also helped out in research and development of new units. One of those assignments took me to Fairbanks, Alaska, in the middle of winter. A hospital there wanted to help locals who had addiction problems that grew very severe in the midst of the long winters. It seems that darkness is a fertilizer for the growth of addiction.

I was living in Southern California at the time, having moved there a few months earlier from Texas. I loved California, with its beaches, its warm weather, and the feel of the sun on my skin every day. During the winter, Southern California residents enjoy some of the most beautiful weather of all when Santa Ana winds come in and dry up everything they roll over and temperatures climb into the eighties and sometimes nineties. So I wasn't too thrilled to leave in the middle of winter, but the thought of going to Alaska for the first time overcame any reluctance I had.

Most visitors see Alaska from cruise ships or on tours that feature viewing of bears, whales, salmon, and eagles. I would see none of that because ten feet of snow tends to slow down the animals. And the fact that it is pitch black almost every minute in winter there prevented me from seeing Alaska as most visitors see and experience it. Incidentally, I would later go there four more times and love every minute of it.

This time I arrived in the middle of the night because

night is just about the only time during the winter. I had not dressed appropriately, carrying only a light jacket for the runs from the buildings to the car. So when the pilot announced it was one of the coldest times there at forty below zero, I was in for a bit of a chill, to say the least.

I rarely check a bag, so I went straight to the rental car desk, signed what had to be signed, and ran out the door to get in the car. As the cold hit me, I wondered why Alaskans would even bother to count the degrees after about minus twenty. Other than that, all I could think of was getting to that car as fast as I could. I located it, threw my one suitcase in the backseat, got in, and slammed the door. It started easily, but as I backed out, I noticed I was tethered to a pole by an electric cord.

Oil freezes in extremely cold weather, so they have to keep the engines warm. The cord was for an idle engine heater. Hesitantly, I opened the door and unplugged the car and wrapped the cord around the hooks in the front. It was so cold I could hardly control the movements of my hands. But I did it and proceeded to follow the directions to the hotel. As I drove down the road, I saw a very strange sight. The cold made the night light look different from any that I had ever seen. It was muted and somehow thicker looking. I know that is an odd description of light, but this seemed thickish.

I checked into the hotel, went to my room, set down my bag, and made my way to the restaurant that I had been told was very good. I knew I would be very satisfied if I could order anything hot. When I entered the restaurant, I was quite surprised to find it full of people. I realized that I had not arrived in the middle of the night, and just because it was dark, people didn't hole up in their houses until March. It was a lively place, and I was shown to a table on the outer rim of the eaters. It was a good place for me to engage in watching people, something I have always loved to do.

I remember one man who entered the restaurant and was seated at a table just above me on an elevated area of tables. Actually, his cologne arrived a couple of seconds before he did. It was very strong and caught my attention immediately. He appeared to be a man of many means, wearing a beautiful blazer with very shiny brass buttons and well-shined Italian loafers that make a man's feet look a size or two smaller than they actually are. And he had good hair. Wealthy people seem to have really good hair.

I was fascinated with him but tried not to stare. My assumption that he was wealthy or at least acted like it was confirmed when I heard him order from the wine steward the best bottle of wine in the house. I don't know how much it cost, but I am certain that even in Fairbanks a nice restaurant had some pretty good wine.

The wine steward went into the back and returned with a bottle of red wine. I chuckled to myself, assuming he had to thaw the wine before bringing it out. I just couldn't get over how cold it was in Alaska. When he presented the wine to the gentleman, there was an accepting nod, and the steward proceeded to uncork the vintage. With the cork removed he poured a bit into his baby rattle–looking medallion hanging from his neck. He sipped it and smiled approvingly as he poured a small amount from the bottle into a very thin wine glass.

I watched as the rich man swished the wine around in his mouth; it looked as though he was gargling. Obviously, it was worth the price, and as he nodded, the wine steward poured him a glass of the nearly black wine. Trying not to be caught staring, I broke away from that little drama and noticed what else was going on in the restaurant. Near the kitchen there was a back exit, and I watched as something unusual began to happen.

While Mr. Rich was obtaining liquid gold, I saw an older woman—wearing a coat that had seen better days—enter. She apparently had spent much time in the elements; her skin was leathery with deep wrinkles, and her hair was very matted. Without making eye contact with anyone, she sat down at a table by the rear door. She placed her elbows on the table and held her head in her hands. I thought of the disparity between her and the man near me. I had a bit of resentment and a lot of jealousy as I wondered what he did to help people like her—not much, I assumed. My assumption, however, had absolutely no basis other than my own bad attitude.

Then someone brought a bowl of soup to the older woman even though she hadn't asked—this was perhaps not the first time she had entered through that exit and taken the table nearest it. She picked up her spoon and ate the soup, her forehead still propped up by her hand. What a contrast of emotion: the woman, looking as down-and-out as one could be, and the well-dressed man, looking up and full of life.

While I had been observing this woman, the wine steward had leaned over to hear the rich man quietly give him directions. The wine steward smiled, picked up the bottle of wine, and put it on a tray, along with a wine glass from the next table. He proceeded to walk across the full and very lively dining room. Surely some of the beautiful people there would have loved the attention of this man. I was not the only one who had noticed his distinguished looks. But the wine steward did not stop at any of their tables.

Instead, he came to the table where the older woman was still eating with her head down. The wine steward leaned over and said something to her, and she immediately lifted her head off her hand and nodded to the steward. He placed the glass from his tray on her table and poured her a glass of wine from the best bottle in the house.

She picked up the glass and looked across the crowded dining room floor until she spotted the wealthy man, standing up with his glass of wine in his hand. When he knew he had her attention, he slowly raised his glass in a toast to her. She tilted her glass toward him in acknowledgment, and together they shared the expensive wine, simultaneously drinking from their glasses.

I could not keep from shedding a couple of tears and swallowing to get the lump out of my throat. I immediately had the feeling that I was there to observe this wonderful drama not by coincidence. It was a message for me if I would take the time to figure it out. So as I pondered the event, several lessons began to emerge.

First of all, the incident was a representation of what

God does for everyone, including me. He will pass up all the beautiful people, just as the wine steward passed them, and he will choose to honor and share the best, his best, with the most unlikely people. He is not a respecter of persons or the door through which we enter a room. He loves us and wants to share the best with us.

This meant a great deal to me since I had struggled with inadequacy for much of my life, thinking everyone else got some kind of rule book, but I did not. They knew how to live, but I had to make it up as I went along. Here was a modern-day example of favor for the most inadequate and unlikely person in the room. It was a reflection of what God had done with Moses, the stuttering murderer; Gideon, the weakest of the weak in his community; David, the adulterer; Zacchaeus, the cheating tax collector; and Paul, the persecutor of Christians. God had used all of these inadequate people who needed to do only one thing. The only thing they needed to do was become willing to share in God's best, which he offered to them.

It was something I needed to understand early in life. And I have watched as it has played out in my life. Early on in college I paid for an abortion, but over the years God has used me to raise millions of dollars for pregnancy and women's centers by speaking at hundreds of fund-raisers.

My past with women was not very pretty. I had objectified them, just as many men from my background do, making women out to be a little less than men. But in spite of that God allowed me to create and start Women of Faith, which has been attended by more than four million women.

I don't have a terminal degree, and I am not a psychologist. Yet I have been able to host a call-in radio show that provides hurting people with biblically sound answers to real-life problems. Many more qualified than me could do that, even though I am, finally, working on a PhD.

I have no seminary degree. I did attend seminary for a couple of years, but I never finished. Now I serve as a teaching pastor of Heartland Church in Indianapolis, Indiana. I'm sure others could do a much better job. Or is that just my inadequate view of myself talking? It still raises its inadequate head every now and then.

And you are reading somewhere around the 110th book I have published (a sign of my never feeling that the last book was good enough). It is quite an accomplishment for me since I had ADD so badly I could not learn a foreign language and got my degree in elementary education because it was the only area that did not require a second language. (I can't imagine that would be the case today.)

What I am trying to say is, that night I saw a real-life version of what God had done in the past and what he was going to do in my future. I am so grateful to have been allowed by God to be involved in the things I have enjoyed so much. It does not make sense except in the mind of God.

Another observation struck me as profound. For this man to bestow this gift in the way he wanted to give it, he needed a wine steward. He could have walked it over to the woman, but that would not have been the same or produced such a profound effect. So he utilized the wine steward, just as God utilizes us to deliver his best to those we serve. I want to be that wine steward. I want to find a place to always serve those who are often overlooked by everyone except God.

I also walked away with the knowledge that sometimes God works best when it is cold and dark. The next day after the encounter, I flew home from Fairbanks with a heart warmer to God and to God's people. I have shared that story with many people because I want them to capture the vision of God passing by the beautiful people to choose the most unlikely to do his work with him.

A final note on this story: Having been raised Southern Baptist, I realize that some readers may be offended by me believing an event from God would involve alcohol. Well, the issue of the rightness or wrongness of drinking is an issue over which good and loving Christians often disagree with other good and loving Christians. I hope you won't get hung up on that issue and miss the message that God perhaps wants you to hear. I hope you won't miss the mission that God is calling you to. I pray that nothing will stand in your way of responding to God in a way that honors his offer of the best there is.

For Deeper Consideration

Here are some questions and concepts for you to consider in solitude. After you have done that, bring your notes to your small group, and be ready to share some of what you discovered as you sought insight from God while you were alone.

1. There are three major characters in this true story: the wealthy man, the older woman, and the wine steward. As

I reflected on the story, I saw the wealthy man representing God, who wants to share his best with us. He has all of the wealth in the world and wants to share it, no matter what we think of him. I saw the older woman representing me, a common person who has been fortunate enough to experience God's grace. I didn't have to be one of the beautiful people for him to want to share his best. Then there was the wine steward. God uses people to deliver his best to others. Which character did you relate to the most? Why did that person reflect more of your life than the others? Are you pleased with the person you are most like, or would you rather it be someone else? Why would that person be a better choice in life?

2. Do you have a similar story of an amazing coincidence or a drama that God orchestrated? Try to remember how the events unfolded and how you felt when you realized God reached out to you. Has that event had any impact on your faith? What could you do so that you never forget some of the wonderful gifts God has given you by way of unexplainable gifts coming together?

3. I was highly critical, envious, and judgmental of the wealthy man. My inadequacy really surfaced in his presence. Do you have some problems that cause certain regrettable feelings to surface? When was the last time those feelings came to the surface? What could you do to resolve those feelings so that you could see everyone as your equal? What life experience do you think had the most influence in developing those attitudes?

Conclusion

I love this story of pain, abandonment, healing, and restoration. It was another example of how God sometimes does supernatural things to assist in our healing and restoration. But even when God moves, we have decisions to make. We must often do the toughest thing we could imagine for restoration to take place. Perhaps this story has motivated you to confront something painful from the past and find a way to reach acceptance. If the need is there for a bold move, I hope you will make it soon.

Solitude and Discussion Guide

The following material is designed for two purposes. One is for you to consider the questions in a time of solitude. Ask God to meet you there as you look at each issue and meditate on what is true and what God is revealing to you. Ask God to be with you as you search deeply for areas that need attention and healing.

The second purpose of the material is for discussion with others. If you have a small group, ask each person to read the book, consider the questions in solitude, and then bring the truth into the group. My hope is that when a person shares, there will be no shame or rejection. And I hope there will be acceptance.

1. Think about your life. Does a situation come to mind when you had a choice to reject or accept someone? What did you do? Would you still make that decision today? Is there anything you could do to make it better or resolve the issues?

2. Everyone has a story, but it might not be the *real* story. Is there a story in your life that you have considered

true, but you are not sure whether it is? What could you do to determine whether you have the real story? Are you willing to make the effort?

3. It is not easy to make something right after many years. Do you have an example of trying to right a wrong and make amends? What are the benefits that have come to you as a result? If you made amends about a certain situation, would it make a difference in someone's life? Is anything holding you back from making that bold move? What would be a first step in that direction?

4. All of us have different childhood experiences even if we live in the same home. The way our parents raise us imprints us in certain ways. Sometimes it leads us to avoid others. Sometimes it leads us to step out and live in commendable ways. Other times it leads us to seek attention in inappropriate ways. What kind of imprint did your parents leave on you? Was it positive or negative? Have you stopped to consider how it has hurt you? Have you considered how going through it might have helped you? Do you ever thank God for the fact that you survived it?

5. Who do you relate to most in the story of Ada Guthrie and Jonathan Rush: mother or son? Why do you choose that person? What feelings do you have as a result of reading about someone who reminds you of yourself? Is there a need for you to forgive yourself for something you did and have never fully resolved? Have you considered that rather than punish you, God wants to restore you and free you? What prevents you from

taking a bigger step toward him and seeking a deeper relationship with him?

6. Sometimes people who are stuck in bitterness and anger believe there is not much to life other than dealing with past hurts and trying to rise above them. Have past hurts prevented you from discovering what God has for your life? What mission do you think you could accomplish? What gifts or skills do you possess that would help you with that mission? What stands in your way of stepping out into a life that will enrich others and leave you fulfilled and excited?

Acknowledgment

Thank you, James Pence, for helping me to communicate the truth.

Steve Arterburn is the host of *New Life Live!*, a radio and television program distributed across the country. He is a best-selling author with more than eight million books in print. He is also the founder of Women of Faith®, a conference attended by more than four million women since its inception. Steve also serves as the teaching pastor of Heartland Church in Indianapolis, Indiana.

If you have a question or a comment for Steve, you can contact him at SArterburn@newlife.com.

The power to heal—physically, mentally, emotionally, spiritually—is in God's hands. But the *choice* to be healed is ours.

Now combined with the complete workbook, this revised and updated edition of *Healing Is a Choice* helps us find the wholeness God desires for us in a practical and prayerful way. Inside, Stephen Arterburn outlines ten choices crucial to receiving healing and ten lies that can prevent us from making them.

ISBN 978-0-7852-3243-8

**A second chance . . . all of us have
needed one at some point in our lives.**

In this revised and updated version of *The God of Second Chances*, Stephen
Arterburn takes us through his own journey of pleasure-seeking and ambi-
tion to a life-changing encounter with the reality of God's grace.

Through his willingness to share his struggles, Arterburn helps us to
confront our failures and reach out for God's restorative touch.

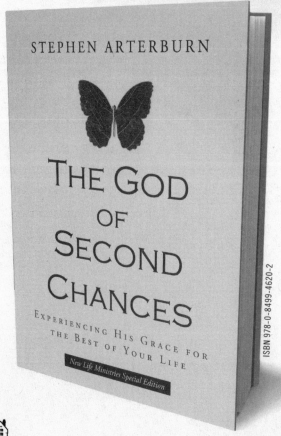